FROM CARTHAGE TO OSLO

A Biography of Al Gore

To my great friend Darius Willis! with thanks, respect and best wishes!

Troy Gipson

MR. TROY GIPSON

May 30, 2014

ISBN: 1478126736
ISBN 13: 9781478126737

Library of Congress Control Number: 2012911926
CreateSpace, North Charleston, SC

Table of Contents:

Dedication

This book is dedicated to my father, the late Claude Gipson Jr., and my good friend the late Jess O'Dear Jr. They will forever be in my memories. I know they would be proud that I finally finished this book..

Introduction

Al Gore has made a lasting impact upon the nation and world through his leadership in public service within the US Government, as an environmental activist in the fight against the climate crisis, and as business leader in the private sector. His rise to world prominence has been a long journey, filled with many successes and some misfortune along the way. During his long political career, Gore was a visionary and is responsible for many important legislative initiatives that, still today, are having a positive impact upon our nation and world. As vice president, Gore served eight distinguished years during one of the most prosperous and peaceful times in our nation's history. He played a leading role in the Clinton White House, heading up the National Performance Review and taking the lead on many of the President's most important legislative issues; including NAFTA, the Medical Leave Act., technology and telecommunications. His influence was so great that he is considered one of the most effective vice presidents in US history. While in Congress, he was rated by several independent congressional groups as one of the ten most effective members. He was the author and sponsor of the National Organ Transplant Act that was signed into law in August of 1984, a law which has saved thousands of lives and helped increase the quality of life for thousands of others.

While serving in Congress, Gore was one of the first members to recognize the dangers of chemicals and pollutants, and he helped write and cosponsored the Super Fund Bill, the landmark legislation on environmental protection. Gore was also ahead of his time in advocating the need for lower health care costs and better quality of medical services, conducting congressional hearings on the issue and many other consumer-friendly issues that have made a difference in all of our lives. Al Gore was also the leading expert in Congress on computer technology, authoring and sponsoring the landmark Supercomputer Network Act of 1986 and the High Performance Computing and Communication Act of 1991. Gore strongly advocated for improvements in the military and national defense arenas and became the leading authority in the US House and Senate on nuclear arms control, praised by both Democrats and Republicans alike. His nuclear arms proposals were even adopted by the United States in its treaty with the former Soviet Union, reducing the number of nuclear weapons stockpiled by the Soviet Union.

Gore became a leading expert on the environment, authoring the book *Earth in the Balance*, which became a best seller and environmental manifesto for the nation and world. In 2000, Gore ran for president, winning the popular vote while narrowly losing in the Electoral College. The election was contested over the controversial vote totals in Florida, with the US Supreme Court ultimately voting 5-4 to halt the Florida vote recount, which ended Gore's hopes of becoming president.

Since leaving public service in 2001, Al Gore has become a renowned crusader on the environment and a successful business entrepreneur. He has authored several best-selling books devoted to the climate crisis, and his documentary film, *An Inconvenient Truth*, was awarded an Oscar in 2007. Gore was also awarded the *Nobel Peace Prize* in 2007 for his efforts in bringing attention to the climate crisis. Today Gore leads and chairs the Climate Reality Project, an organization that is having a major impact upon the climate crisis. Gore also serves on the Board of Directors at Apple and is chairman and co-founder of Current TV; chairman of Generation Investment Management; and an advisor to Google. Gore has reached a new plateau, and has created a position of influence that reaches far beyond politics, and extends across the world.

Al Gore behind the scenes is a complex man who possesses great intellect and common sense, who can talk and relate to a farmer, while fitting in perfectly with Ivy League professors and NASA engineers. He is focused and driven and can sometimes be reserved and remote, but has a humorous side not often seen in public. He has very high demands and expectations, yet he is also very forgiving and extremely loyal. He is also the smartest person I have ever known in my life. In all my years working in aerospace and politics, I have never met anyone who can come close to this man on an intellectual level.

The idea to write this book was conceived shortly after Gore was elected vice president of the United States in November 1992. I had been a Gore supporter since his initial foray into politics, when he ran for Congress in 1976. I was a young boy in junior high school, wearing a body cast while recovering from back surgery earlier that year. It was during the summer of his first campaign when I first met him, and he seemed to be drawn to me. Maybe he felt sorry for me, or maybe he just sensed that I really liked him. Whatever the reason, the fact remains that we became friends and I became fixated on his political career. I was so inspired by him that I decided to study political science at Middle Tennessee State University. It was during my college years when I served as a congressional intern to Gore, on two different occasions, and through the years, I worked in all of his political campaigns, doing everything from handing out campaign brochures in his first race to later organizing fundraisers, always looking to use my influence to persuade potential supporters. And because of all this, to this day my family and close friends associate me with Al Gore. But in reality I was just one of many who believed in his political ideas, and thus closely followed his political career. In so doing I have been able to formulate an extensive knowledge of Al Gore including his early life and political career. His career has been a long journey, one that has had many twists and turns, and that requires careful examination and understanding.

There are many reasons that I wrote this book, but foremost I wanted to tell a story about the other side of Al Gore, the one that most of the world does not know. While there have been several books written about the former vice president, there has never been a complete and historical account of him as told by someone close to him. In so doing I have tried to provide the most accurate and comprehensive account of this man to date, from the days before he became famous, to behind the scenes of his political career.

I wrote this book as a reporter who investigates and researches the facts, simply reviewing the history and events in the life of Al

Gore, adding the recollections of many people who knew him, while also adding my own personal accounts and opinion. My personal experiences with Al Gore in his political campaigns and as an intern allowed me access to him and his staff. I took notes on many occasions during the past thirty years whenever I would meet or accompany him, and accumulated personal files of information in the process. In addition, I selected and researched newspaper and magazine articles, television interviews, speeches, and political campaign materials. Yet it was my own personal interface with and knowledge of Al Gore that allowed me to outline, analyze, and write the book. I sincerely hope this book will be of value and interest to both the causal reader and political scientist.

TROY GIPSON

Quotes from others

"Al Gore is the kind of leader these times require. Not as President—God and the Electoral College have given him a different job. As it happens, Al is at work repositioning his country from the inside out as a leader in clean energy; and along the way restoring faith in the U. S. as a moral powerhouse that can lead a great, global spiritual revival as the temperature rises."

BONO, TIME MAGAZINE

"Al brings an incredible wealth of knowledge and wisdom to Apple from having helped run the largest organization in the world—as a Congressman, Senator and our 45th Vice President."

STEVE JOBS

"Al Gore helped me a lot in the early days, encouraging me to keep making hard decisions and put them behind me, and giving me a continuing crash course in how Washington works." Al understood Congress and the Washington culture far better than I did. Most important, I thought he would be a good President if something happened to me."

PRESIDENT BILL CLINTON, MY LIFE

"Al Gore was on our set recently, and I watched him walk from one side of the room to the other, shaking hands and greeting each and every person there, from the highest level executives to the entry-level secretary. Treating everyone the same says so much about who you are in your heart."

WENDY WALKER, PRODUCER CNN

CHAPTER 1

The Beginning

Al Gore phoned me one afternoon in early January 2010. He was returning a call that I had made to his office a few weeks earlier. I was down and out, having experienced recent losses in my life, and I just wanted to talk to him. As he answered the phone, he politely said in a deep-toned voice, "Troy, this is Al Gore. How are you doing?" I answered, "Hi, Mr. Vice President. How are you?" It was as if we had spoken only a few days ago, but actually it had been a while since we had last spoken to or seen each other. Then he said, "I understand that your father passed away and that your mother is now in a nursing home. I'm very sorry to hear that." I thanked him for calling me and told him I just needed to talk to him. He said he understood, and then after telling him about my current situation, I told him how heartbroken I was about the 2000 presidential election and how I always wanted to call him Mr. President. Vice President Gore then said to me, in a rather solemn voice, "Well, Troy, I wish that it were so, but it isn't." I then told him that I would like to see him and talk to him in private. He said, "Well, I'll have Beth [his administrative assistant] set something up." As I hung up the phone, I felt elated, the same emotion that I had experienced many times during the long political career of Al Gore. Only this time it was different, and, for the first time, I gained a sense of just how much the American people and the world had lost by not having this man as president. A simple phone call had spoken a million words, in ways that can be understood only by being on the other end of the phone, talking to the man who had seen his life's dream fade away on that fateful day in November, in the closest, most bizarre presidential election in the nation's history.

If ever there were a man destined and raised to be a leader, Al Gore was such a man. Had he grown up during medieval times, he most certainly would have been a prince, but in our system of government, he had to settle for a less glamorous title—politician. Like the medieval prince, Gore was born into power and royalty, and from his first day in kindergarten to the day of the final decision of the US Supreme Court in *Bush v. Gore*, Al Gore was groomed to be president.

Al Gore was born in Washington, DC, on March 31, 1948, to Albert and Pauline Gore. At the time, Gore's father was a United States congressman from Carthage, Tennessee who had been elected to Congress in 1938 and was serving in the 4th[th] Congressional District. Gore also had an older sister, Nancy, who he looked up to with great respect and admiration. While his father was working in Congress, Gore and his family lived in an apartment at the Fairfax Hotel on Embassy Row in Fairfax, Virginia. Embassy Row was a place where the sons and daughters of senators and congressmen lived alongside the rich, elite, and powerful. And while they wanted their children to experience the cosmopolitan life in Washington, with its many cultural and political offerings, they also insisted that their children experience life in the rural country with it's natural set-tings. So when Congress was out of session during the summer, the Gore's would return to their farm in Carthage, Tennessee. Carthage is a small, rural town located in the upper Cumberland region of north central Tennessee. It is a landscape of hills and valleys situated between the Cumberland and Caney Fork rivers, with US Highway 70 connecting Carthage with Nashville, approximately 46 miles to the west, and Cookeville 36 miles to the east. The people, both hard-working and God-fearing, typically work on farms, in factories, or in service-related jobs. It was settled by early European-Americans who migrated there because of the rivers and natural boundaries. It was in this small rural and humble setting of rolling hills and rivers that young Albert would spend his summers hauling hay and doing chores around the farm. His father and mother wanted to ensure that he was brought up to understand and appreciate hard work. Of course, that was what was expected of young people back in the 1950s. It was a time when people worked hard, whether they were the son of a farmer or a prominent senator. In the case of Al Gore Jr., it was both.

The Gores had a large 260-acre stretch of farm, along the Caney Fork River, where they raised hay, tobacco, and their famous Angus cattle, the best stock in the nation. Young Al would enjoy fishing and swimming in the Caney Fork River and swimming in the Carthage city pool when he was not working on the farm. He also made friends with the local sons and daughters of cattle farmers, store owners, and fellow churchgoers, fitting in perfectly with the people of rural Carthage. Al Gore Jr. also demonstrated a superior intellect at an early age and was naturally gifted. His parents instilled an intense desire and ambition in Gore from his early childhood, prodding him to be the best and smartest, and teaching him to honor his elders and to treat all people with kindness and respect, regardless of class or race. That spark that was lit by his parents turned out to become an intense fire within his soul, which would consume him throughout his life. It was the lightning rod that would allow him to become so focused and driven, which would eventually lead to his ascension into politics and public service.

Gore's sister, Nancy, was also very intelligent and grew to become distinguished in her own right. She graduated from Vanderbilt University, volunteered for the US Peace Corps, and later met and married Frank Hungar, from Greeneville, Mississippi, who eventually became a lawyer. Frank grew very close to the Gore family, especially to Al Gore Jr., who immediately connected with him. Frank was like the brother that Gore never had and ultimately became an advisor and close confidant to Gore throughout his entire political career.

Gore's father was now a very powerful United States senator from Tennessee. Elected in 1952, he had defeated the longtime incumbent, Senator Kenneth McKeller of Memphis, one of the most powerful and longest-serving members of the Senate. Albert Gore Sr. was raised in rural Overton County, Tennessee, in "hillbilly country," and he worked his way up to superintendent of Smith County Schools before finally running for Congress in 1938. The elder Gore was a very intelligent yet common man, with a folksy, southern accent, and the charm to make people like him. Senator Albert Gore was also a national statesman and maverick politician, who fought for the common people and, at times, supported controversial and unpopular issues. He was a man of conviction and principle and believed in voting his conscience and doing what he thought was right for the state of Tennessee and the nation. He was extremely popular with liberals, friends with many conservatives in both political parties, and had worked well with numerous presidents, including Franklin Roosevelt, Harry Truman, Dwight Eisenhower, John Kennedy, and Lyndon Johnson, during his long career spanning almost four decades. Indeed it was rather difficult to put a single label on Senator Albert Gore, because at times he would go against the wishes of his own Democratic Party. In 1956 he was one of only three southern democratic US senators who refused to sign the segregationist Southern Manifesto, demonstrating his desire to see all people treated equally, regardless of class or race. Senator Gore was so popular with the Democrats that he almost became the Democratic nominee for vice president in 1956, when Adlai Stevenson won the nomination for president. Indeed, Senator Albert Gore Sr. would have a profound effect upon his son, and his votes of conviction in the Senate would always teach the younger Gore valuable lessons on politics and government, such was the case with Senator Gore's stances on the Vietnam conflict and the segregation issue.

Al Gore Jr's mother, Pauline Lafollette Gore, was very intelligent and distinguished in her own right. Not only was she a lawyer, she was also one of the first women to graduate from Vanderbilt Law School, which was quite an accomplishment at the time. She also managed her husband's political campaigns for Congress and the

Senate, and was his biggest supporter and advisor. She met Albert Gore Sr. while waiting tables in a hotel restaurant in downtown Nashville, where he had been attending night law school.

Pauline Gore would have a big influence on Al Gore Jr. throughout his life and career, and Gore naturally acquired some of her talents and instincts. His mother was very pragmatic and cautious, whereas his father, Senator Gore, was more abrupt and stubborn in his beliefs. Senator Gore Sr. was never afraid to run against the public opinion, as he tackled many liberal causes in a way that was not always aligned with the views of his constituents. Pauline Gore, by her own admission, stated that she tried to teach young Al Jr. to be more like her when it came to politics. "Al by nature is more of a pragmatist than his father. As am I," she told the *Los Angeles Times*. "I tried to persuade Albert not to butt at a stone wall just for the sheer joy of butting…if there's no chance of victory, there's no sense in bloodying yourself," she said.[1] Al Gore acquired traits from both of his parents, with his people skills and political charm from his father and his intense focus and discipline from his mother; while he inherited his extraordinary intelligence from both. Although Gore's parents had different personalities, they shared a common affection and admiration for their children. Moreover, they both demanded that their children grow up living a normal life, experiencing both the hard work on the farm in Carthage, and the cosmopolitan life of Washington, with its many cultural offerings. In young Al Gore, they could foresee a future senator, or even president. Their focus on the prize would never waver throughout the rest of their lives.

In 1965 Al Gore Jr. graduated from St. Albans, an elite, preparatory boy's school in Washington, DC. St. Albans is a graceful place, with grand stone buildings, lush green lawns, and an Ivy League look and feel. The school was a very strict and ridged place, with its goal to instill discipline, character, morals, and honor. Gore was well respected by his classmates and teachers, made excellent grades, fit in, and made friends with almost everyone he came in contact with. He was also a good athlete and played basketball and football at St. Albans, with basketball being his best sport. Gore later entered

---

[1] Karen Tumulty, *Los Angeles Times Magazine*, August 21, 2000

Harvard, where he studied political science, and there he became friends with a group of other prominent young people who would later become famous in their own right, including actor Tommy Lee Jones. By all accounts, including those of his professors and friends at Harvard, he was one of the best and brightest and took his studies seriously. He also was applauded for his good manners and likeability, while showing superior intellectual ability. While at Harvard, Gore, like most of the young men and women of his generation, demonstrated against the war in Vietnam; he even attended a few campaign rallies during Eugene McCarthy's run for the presidency. Gore graduated summa cum laude in 1969, and soon after he volunteered for the US Army. As fate would have it, Gore served a brief stint in Vietnam as a reporter. It is ironic that while Gore was serving in Vietnam, his father, adamantly opposed to the war, was making speeches against the war on the floor of the US Senate. While Al easily could have chosen not to serve, he was proud to call himself a "patriot" for fighting for his country, even though, like his father, he had reservations about the extent and duration of the war.

Al volunteered for the U.S. Army in August of 1969 and received basic training shortly thereafter. After his military training, he was stationed at Ft. Rucker, Alabama. Then on May 10, 1970, Gore married the former Mary Elizabeth "Tipper" Aitcheson, at the Washington National Cathedral. They had met while Al was attending St. Albans School in Washington D.C. After their marriage, Al and Tipper moved to Ft. Rucker, Alabama where Gore was stationed until January 2, 1971, when he was deployed to Vietnam, where he would spend the next year. After his Army service, the Gore's moved to Nashville, Tennessee, where they would spend the next few years, with Al attending divinity school at Vanderbilt University, while Tipper worked as a photographer. During this time they enjoyed their work and also took trips across the country, driving from Tennessee and camping out in various national parks along the way. Al and Tipper both enjoyed the outdoors and nature, and they cherished these long trips into the great lands of the United States[2]. This was a period in Al Gore's life where he was trying to search for

---

2 Albert Gore, An Inconvient Truth (2006)

answers to some questions he had about society and institutions, and was one of the main reasons that he decided to enter divinity school. He also attended law school for a brief time.

The Gore's first child, Karena, was born on August 6, 1973, and in the same year, Al joined the Nashville Tennessean, a major newspaper in Nashville, Tennessee. He began his career as a reporter covering local politics, where he developed into a very successful journalist. Al later became an investigative reporter, becoming an aggressive and effective reporter who uncovered corruption within state and local governments. He genuinely enjoyed being a reporter and the demanding but rewarding aspects of the profession. One of his fellow reporters at the Tennessean, Jim O'Hara, would later recall: "Al approached reporting as he approaches everything else— he worked hard at it. He was extremely tenacious and hated mistakes. He was a careful reporter, somebody who wanted to take the time he knew was necessary to a story. Needless to say, on a daily newspaper, that drove editors up the wall."[3] Gore also became good friends with Tennessean John Seigenthaler, the legendary publisher and editor. While working at the Tennessean, Gore would learn some hard lessons about how corrupt politics could be, and he seemed to be turned off by the political environment that was surrounding the nation. During this time he also attended law school at night, considering a career as a lawyer. However politics seemed to be far from his mind.

In early 1976, word started surfacing across Tennessee that longtime Congressman Joe L. Evins was contemplating retiring from his 4th Congressional District seat. Evins was a very popular congressman from Smithville who had accomplished many great things for the people of his district during his twenty-year career. Nevertheless, it was finally time for him to retire and pass the torch to someone younger. Al Gore was still working as an investigative reporter for the *Tennessean* at the time, but when his friend called him with the news about Evins, he didn't hesitate. After all, it was Al's time to finally run for his first elective office. The announcement didn't come as a surprise to Gore's colleagues at the *Tennessean*,

---

3 Amy Lynch, "Senator Superman", Nashville Magazine, March 1985.

as they had seen firsthand Gore's quick grasp of politics and also his interest and desire to make a difference in government. Having witnessed firsthand how corrupt politics could be, this undoubtedly played a role in Gore's decision to run for Congress. "I was in law school, finishing up my second year, when Joe Evins made a surprise announcement. I got a call from a friend at the *Tennessean* saying that he'd gotten advance word that Monday morning's paper would have the announcement of Joe Evins' retirement. I put the phone on the hook and turned to Tipper and said 'I think I'm gonna run for Congress. But it surprised me that I knew. We hadn't really talked about it, and we hadn't been to any political rallies, we hadn't been actively involved in the party. But I made that decision on the spur of the moment and three days later I walked out on the courthouse steps in Carthage and announced my candidacy."[4] Gore read a prepared speech that outlined the theme of his campaign and the issues that he wanted to work on if he were elected to Congress. He was very focused and talked about populist ideas, which is what the 4th District wanted to hear. It would be the beginning of a long journey in Al Gore's political career.

---

4 Ibid.

CHAPTER 2

The Race for Congress: 1976

In the spring of 1976, I was a young twelve year old, wearing a body cast while recovering from back surgery earlier that year. I was staying with my aunt and uncle at their general store in Oak Grove, in rural Franklin County, Tennessee. One afternoon, a car pulled up outside the store. A tall, dark haired man, got out of the car with a quick jump. He was dressed is a navy blue suit, blue shirt, and red tie, which would later become his uniform. He moved up quickly to the farmers who were sitting on the storefront porch and began to shake their hands. After carefully talking to everyone, he then went inside the store. This is when I first saw him. He came up to me and put out his hand and said, "Hello, I'm Albert Gore Jr. and I'm running for Congress." I shook his hand and said, "very nice to meet you." I was awestruck! It was like meeting a movie star. Even back then he had that rare ability to walk into a room full of people and light it up with his presence. I knew right away that I was meeting someone special, and in my heart, I just knew this nice man was going to be famous one day, instantly realizing that I had to get involved in his campaign for Congress. If he had been going to the moon, I would have probably followed him. The fact that he was running for Congress was just incidental. We both seemed to instantly connect with each other. Maybe he felt sorry for me because I was wearing the cast, or perhaps he sensed that would support him. Whatever the reason, the fact remains we became friends, and I became fixated on his political career.

At the time, I vaguely knew him. I was familiar with his father, former Senator Albert Gore Sr., and had met him at a cattle show at my uncle's farm several years earlier. Later on, my sister told me that in fact Al Gore Jr. was also with his father that day at my uncle's farm. And so everyone knew who Al Gore Jr. was because of his father, and that would serve to be both an asset but also a burden in his campaign for Congress. Critics of Al's father would try to convince the voters to oppose him.

Senator Albert Gore Sr. had served the nation with distinction for over thirty-eight years as a populist congressman and senator, and was considered one of the best and brightest senators in the nation. He was the Senate sponsor of the National Interstate System, which was signed into law by President Eisenhower in the 1950s, and a supporter of civil and equal rights. The Grey Fox, as he was affectionately known by many supporters, had also voted to support the Voting Rights Act of 1965, which gave all people the right to vote regardless of race. But Albert Gore Sr. had been voted out of office in a bitter election in 1970, losing to candy company mogul Bill Brock of Chattanooga. There were many reasons for the defeat. Tennessee had been a solid Democratic state since reconstruction, but it had voted for Richard Nixon in 1968, and like most of the southern states, there were issues that President Richard Nixon and the Republican Party were using (civil rights, the Vietnam War, law and order, etc.) to try to divide the people in the Democratic Party across the south, and it worked.[5] By 1970 Tennessee had become more of a conservative state, its voters still struggling with social issues like civil and equal rights, while they continued to support less government and taxes. Beyond that, most voters in Tennessee

---

5 Albert Gore, The Eye of the Storm, (1970), 93-95, others selected

were committed to the war in Vietnam to a limited extent and were uncomfortable with the changes in society that the younger generation was leading. Knowing all of this, Senator Albert Gore Sr. decided that he would stay out of the public eye during his son's race for Congress and would help behind the scenes only. He feared that if he made public speeches on his son's behalf, the voters would focus on him and the issues that had cost him his re-election to the Senate, thus detracting attention from his son's race.

Al Gore Jr. began his race for Congress with instant name recognition and a strong base of support from his father's political contacts, giving him an advantage over most of the other candidates in the race. The 4th Congressional District was a rural area of Tennessee, consisting of twenty-five counties, stretching across the north-eastern part of the state next to the Kentucky border, and down into the middle and southern end, near the border of Alabama. Its citizens and voters were populist and moderate, supporters of guns, low taxes, and military, and social programs like social security and veteran's affairs. In short, the district was the typical southern congressional district, which had voted for the Democrats since the days of Franklin Roosevelt and the New Deal, the same area of Tennessee where Cordell Hull and Al Gore's father had both served many years before. This was an area that didn't have inside plumbing and running water until the Tennessee Valley Authority (TVA) came along through the public works program during the Great Depression, and thus its people continued to vote for the Democrats because of the progress that had been made in their lives.

The 4th District consisted of cities like Murfreesboro, Gallatin, and Cookeville, and small towns like Carthage, Decherd, and Manchester. But it mostly consisted of small rural communities like Difficult, Defeated, and Oak Grove. The citizens were hard-working and God-fearing, consisting mostly of middle to lower class working families, with its population predominately white, Anglo-Saxon, and Protestant. Most of the people worked either as laborers, farmers, teachers, or in service-related and factory jobs. This was the setting in which Al Gore Jr. would enter his first race for elected office.

In addition to Al Gore Jr., eight other candidates were vying for an opportunity to represent the 4th Congressional District, including

State Representative Stanley Rogers of Manchester. Rogers was a powerful state representative and Democratic Majority Leader who had been in office for several years and had become very popular in the Democratic Party establishment. He would quickly prove to be the biggest obstacle to Al Gore's dream of becoming a congressman. Other candidates included Ben McFarlane, an attorney from Murfreesboro, and Tommy Cutrer, the country music announcer from Hendersonville. The race, however, would ultimately come down to two candidates: Gore and Rogers.

Stanley Rogers had forged a formidable political base in his brief tenure in state politics and was generally well liked in the surrounding counties of his district. He would try to use that to his advantage. Rogers' strategy against Gore was to try to paint him as a young, inexperienced, liberal elitist, whose political philosophy was out of sync with the people of rural Tennessee. Rogers railed at the federal bureaucracy, TVA's cost plus contracts, and Big Government, while Gore's political philosophy was moderate, in keeping with the traditional character of the 4th District. While the 4th District was solidly Democratic, its voters were still primarily moderate to conservative on most issues. Therefore, Al knew in order to beat Stanley Rogers, he would have to convince the people that he was in fact a moderate on the issues.

Gore's campaign printed up brochures that outlined his stances on the issues. The first issue that he listed in the campaign brochure was gun control. On this issue, Gore said, "I am opposed to any additional efforts to force homeowners, law-abiding citizens and sportsmen to feed their names and the serial numbers of their guns into the federal government's computers for registration. Any gun control law enacted by Congress should be aimed at criminals, not law-abiding gun owners. The effort to register all guns is typical of attempts to solve real problems with cosmetic, bureaucratic remedies. Such laws invite massive civil disobedience and offer only false hopes and more paperwork. I strongly favor law enforcement, crime prevention and stiffer penalties for crimes committed with firearms."[6] Gore also talked about Big Government, stating that "Washington must realize that there are limits to what the federal government can do, and what we ought to ask the federal government to do. Once a bureaucracy is set up, there seems to be no way to get rid of it—even if it is no longer needed. I have proposed a 'Sunset Law' requiring the automatic dissolution of federal agencies if the bureaucrats cannot justify their continued employment, in public hearings before the Congress, on a five-year cycle. If they are not doing the job, then we have found a way to cut the budget." On the environment, Gore was already thinking ahead. "Only in recent years have we learned the fact that our environment can be irrevocably spoiled unless we take steps to improve and maintain its purity. We must find and preserve the delicate balance between the environmental necessities and the need to continue economic and industrial progress. I will constantly work toward development of good conservation practices. These are just a few of the issues I hope to discuss with you during this campaign. When elected, I intend to be available to you at all times to help you and work with you. I hope you will join with me in this campaign. Together, we can rekindle the spirit of America."[6]

The campaign was led by a small group of young but talented volunteers, including Johnny Hayes, an insurance salesman from Hendersonville who would prove to be a key figure in the campaign and serve in future Gore campaigns. The campaign treasurer was Walter King Robinson Jr. But of course Gore's greatest campaign assets were members of his family, including his wife Tipper, his father and mother, and his sister Nancy Gore Hunger and her husband, Frank. They were all actively involved in advising Gore in his campaign and making campaign stops all across the 4th District. Gore also had the support of many of his father's former supporters along the winding 4th District. Realizing that he could count on a strong base of support throughout the district, Gore quickly organized campaign organizations and chairmen in each county. The Gore campaign then began to identify the key counties that would ultimately decide the outcome of the election. It became apparent that Rogers' stronghold was the adjoining counties near his hometown of Manchester, which included Bedford, Franklin, Lincoln, Warren, and Coffee (his home county). To offset Rogers' advantage in these counties, the Gore campaign countered with their own campaign

---

6 Gore for Congress Campaign Brochure, 1976

strategy, which was simple and to the point. It required Gore to carry the northern counties of the Upper Cumberland by a huge margin, limiting the margin of defeat in Rogers' home base, while gaining an advantage in the so-called neutral counties, where neither candidate had a clear advantage. To accomplish this, the campaign made a direct assault on Rogers' home-base counties, quickly organizing campaign organizations in each of the counties. All of these counties had key Gore family friends and contracts, with many having campaigned for Al's father in 1938, when he first ran for Congress.

The Gore campaign then went into full throttle, with door-to-door campaigning across all of the counties in the district.

Al would spend his days on the road campaigning, making stops at courthouses, country stores, county fairs, and private fundraisers. I vividly recall one of Gore's congressional campaign fundraisers held in Winchester at the Scenic Restaurant, owned by Buddy and Geraldine Perry. The Scenic was the place to be for all local and state politicians running for office, and Gore was no exception. During the event, a crowd of over one hundred people were gathered to meet and greet the man from Carthage. Al walked into the restaurant with a quick stride, smiling widely while shaking hands with each person. He had somewhat of a southern drawl in his voice, but commanding, and always carefully articulating each word he spoke. The crowd was made up of businessmen, farmers, lawyers, union workers, the elderly and young people. Gore worked the crowd like he was a preacher greeting his brethren. Then after he had greeted the crowd of voters and volunteers, he went to the back of the building, where he made a short, formal speech. He outlined briefly the key concepts that he held believed Government was about, and also shared his views on the issues that he wanted to work on in Congress. The reception was a big success, and one of hundreds that he held all over the 4th District during the campaign. It was in these small settings that he connected with the voters, and they ultimately made the difference in the race.

His campaign volunteers and friends would also go door to door handing out campaign brochures, putting up campaign signs, and affixing bumper stickers to cars. One time, I rode in the car with Al Gore and his campaign aide, Carrey Wofford, on a campaign swing in Winchester, stopping at the old H.G. Hills Store near the courthouse square. Al shook every hand and said hello to everyone he came in contact with. Even back then, in his first campaign, he looked like a seasoned politician working the crowds, with his charm and friendly demeanor. It seemed to be Gore's destiny that he would naturally become a politician, as he looked and played the part perfectly. He campaigned tirelessly across the rural 4th District of Tennessee, frequently spending the night with campaign supporters before rising early the next day to make another swing of campaign stops. He also packed light, carrying only a couple of shirts, one pair of shoes, and usually only one navy blue striped suit, typical of how Gore was raised to be modest. By the end of the campaign, it became apparent that the race would be won by either Al Gore or Stanley Rogers. Both campaigns blitzed the television airwaves and newspapers with campaign ads all across the district, with the other candidates in the race unable to raise enough money for television campaign ads. Finally, after eight exhaustive months of campaigning, it was now time for the voters to decide Gore's fate.

On the eve of the election, both Gore and Rogers predicted they would win the race. Gore stated that he predicted he would win nineteen of the district's twenty-five counties, based on polling from each of his county campaign chairmen. He called his prediction a "cautious estimate," and also said his campaign chairmen believed he would run strong in five other counties. The election was held on August 4, 1976. Throughout the rolling hills and valleys of the 4th district in Tennessee, men and women were voting in courthouses, schools, and stores, in an exercise of power shared by the citizens, some whom were farmers, laborers, students, and the elderly. Shortly after the polls closed, the results began to flicker in to the campaign headquarters.

As the vote totals mounted on the television screens, the results showed Al Gore surging ahead over Stanley Rogers. In the district's northern counties, Gore was ringing up a substantial margin in his home-base counties, winning by a margin of more than 2 to 1 over Rogers. In Putnam County, Gore tallied 2,424 votes, while Rogers carried 1,540. Al Gore carried Wilson County, winning 4086–2107 over Rogers. In Gore's hometown of Carthage, in Smith County,

Gore beat Rogers 3004–619. In Clay County Gore beat Rogers 1,023 to 388. Tommy Cutrer, the popular country music announcer, carried his home county, Sumner, garnering 5,661 votes to Gore's 3,633 and Rogers'1,252. Ben McFarlane, the attorney from Murfreesboro, won his home county, Rutherford, collecting 3,872 votes to Gore's 2,149 and Rogers' 1,506. This meant that the race would come down to the southern counties, specifically the neighboring counties next to Coffee County, which included Franklin, Bedford, Lincoln, Marshall, Moore, Grundy, and Warren. Stanley Rogers would need to carry all of those counties by a wide margin in order to offset Al Gore's vote totals in the Upper Cumberland area. As the votes continued to be counted, Rogers won his home county, Coffee, tallying 5,621 votes to Gore's 1,376, and also beat Gore in Bedford County, winning 2094–1511. In Franklin County, Rogers beat Gore 3222–2224, and in Lincoln County he outpaced Gore 1960–1334. Rogers also won in Warren County, 3231–1715, and in Grundy County, 666–533. However, Gore defeated Rogers in Marshall County, 1480–1168. While Rogers had won the majority of the southern counties, he had not gained enough of a margin over Gore to offset the results in the Upper Cumberland counties of the district. Slowly, as the hours went by, results from the last of the precincts reporting were now in, and Gore was still ahead. Shortly before 9:00 p.m. (EST), Al Gore Jr. was declared the winner over Stanley Rogers.[7]

After all of the ballots were counted, Al Gore had defeated Stanley Rogers by 3,479 votes. The campaign strategy had worked as planned, with the results almost exactly as the Gore campaign had predicted. Gore heavily carried his home-base counties of the Upper Cumberland Region, while running close in the counties where Rogers had won. In the counties outside each candidate's home base, it appears that Al's name recognition gave him an advantage over Rogers. These counties gave Gore close to a 4000-vote advantage. Overall, the final results showed Al Gore with 37,600 votes, Stanley Rogers with 34,121, and Tommy Cutrer, finishing

---

7 Tennessee Blue Book, 1978-79

third, with 19,856 votes. The remaining six candidates tallied a combined 26,069 votes.[8]

It is generally believed that the influx of candidates may have cost Gore more votes than Rogers, the theory being that McFarlane and Cutrer took more votes away in the populous counties of Rutherford and Sumner—two counties in which Gore's father had strong ties—than would otherwise have been the case. Al also ran strongly in the rural areas of the district, just as his father had done throughout his political career, and it seemed that the rural voters had made the difference in the outcome. In some ways, the narrow margin of victory seemed to instill in Gore closeness with his loyal supporters, giving him a sense that his victory was due in large part to their hard work. It also instilled in him the need to maintain close contact with his constituents, and for that, Gore had a plan.

8 Ibid.

CHAPTER 3

House of Representatives: 1977–1985

After a long and tiring campaign, it was time for Al Gore to begin his new job as congressman of Tennessee's 4th District. Gore was sworn into office on January 4, 1977, in the Capitol in Washington, DC. A reception was held for his family and supporters shortly thereafter, from 2:00 p.m. to 5:00 p.m., in the Rayburn House office building next to the Capitol.[9] Now the real race was on for Gore. He had lots of new ideas about how Congress and the federal government should work, and he was very anxious to get started and immerse himself into his new job. Almost immediately after the election, Gore began to show signs of becoming a populist crusader like his father, and he began to select issues that were safe and popular with the voters of his district. What was different about the younger

---

9 Al Gore Jr. Constitutional Oath in US House of Representatives, Fourth District of Tennessee, January 4, 1977 (Original Copy of Invitation)

Gore, however, was the way in which he communicated and stayed in touch with his constituents. Gore had promised in the campaign that he would stay in constant contact with his constituents through his district offices and town hall meetings, so he immediately established congressional offices in Carthage, Cookeville, Gallatin, Murfreesboro, and Winchester. The Carthage office would serve as the 4th District Headquarters, with Washington being the base. In each of the district offices, Gore had staff members who acted on his behalf. He also accumulated a top notch staff in his Washington and District Offices. The staff would receive and answer thousands of letters and phone calls from constituents, helping them with a wide range of issues, such as Social Security, Veterans Affairs, and other federal programs. For Gore, this direct communication with the people allowed him the opportunity to help his constituents with issues that were vitally important. During the first few years in Congress, Gore would personally read and sign each letter that was received from his constituents, a laborious task. Moreover, he seemed to have more energy than the average politician. He would sometimes work fourteen-hour days in Washington, and sleep no more than four or five hours a night. Then, on most weekends, he would spend his time working, reading, and telephoning constituents. Even when Congress was in session, he would sometimes fly back to Nashville and spend the entire weekend, driving around the district and conducting town hall meetings with constituents. Gore seemed to be everywhere, and the speed and efficiency with which he conducted his work baffled even the most seasoned politicians. It was apparent early on that Gore had the skills and talent to become an effective legislator. He had a keen sense of the issues and the political instinct to recognize opportunities for improvement within the Federal Government. Many politicians spend entire careers without adopting universal and meaningful legislation. Amazingly, Gore was able to author and sponsor more than a dozen major bills that would prove to be both much needed and widely popular with the people. This unique ability to create universally accepted legislation also enabled Al Gore to be re-elected with little to no opposition throughout his entire career in the House and Senate.

The open town hall meetings would prove to be the key to maintaining Gore's success and popularity throughout his career. Gore's office would mail out in advance small post cards to the constituents in the 4th District. A typical open-meeting announcement might read, "Albert Gore, Jr. to Hold Open Meeting in Franklin County/ Decherd. In an effort to make representative democracy work the way it is supposed to work, I am holding an open meeting on Monday, April 7th, from 4:00 until 5:00 p.m., at the Decherd City Hall. If you have any ideas or suggestions on how to improve the operation of the federal government, please come and let me know about them. Sincerely, Albert Gore Jr." [10]

Gore conducted his 1000th open meeting in Difficult, Tennessee, on April 24, 1982. "Hey, how y'all doing," said the man who emerged wearing a blue suit and tie that stood out among the bib overalls and other work clothes. "Gore, accompanied by three aides, led the crowd of mostly farmers to a pasture adjoining the rustic grocery, where a batch of folding chairs, set up for the occasion, was soon filled. There he fielded a wide array of questions from people who, before his arrival, had been talking mostly about crops and the weather. He fielded questions, on topics ranging from Social Security to the economy, without missing a beat. "I had my 500th meeting in Lucky, Tennessee, so I figured I'd have my 1,000[th] in Difficult. You're welcome to join me at my next one – at Flynn's Lick." In these open meetings, Gore would more often than not run into people who had known his father, Senator Albert Gore Sr., with many having campaigned and voted for him. Gore had found a way to keep in touch with the people. He didn't invent the town hall open meetings, but he sure made them become popular once again. At the time, it was not common to find congressmen driving around during the summer in temperatures near one-hundred degrees, spending twelve to fourteen hours a day talking to their constituents.[11]

The open meetings also allowed Al to uncover issues that were of concern to the public. One such case occurred in May 1980, in Murfreesboro, Tennessee. As recounted in the *Tennessean*, "Gore

---

10 Open Meeting – US Congressman Albert Gore, Jr., 1982 (Original Copy)
11 Mark Schwedt, Tennessean, April 25, 1982

was addressing an American Legion youth group for girls when he asked them whether they believed a nuclear war would be fought in their lifetime". To Gore's astonishment nearly ninety percent of the group raised their hands. When Congressman Gore asked if there was anything they believed could be done about it about five hands went up." "I was shocked," Al would later say. From that day forward Gore would set out to become a national expert in the field of nuclear arms control. "I began to build a conviction in my mind that I would do whatever I could to learn about the arms race and to find ways to deal with it,"[12] Gore said. Some of the legislation that Al Gore dealt with in his early career was incredibly sophisticated and complex. In hindsight it is fascinating to see that he was very much ahead of his time on many of the issues that dominate the political landscape today. Health care was one of those issues. In January 1979, Gore sent out a letter to the constituents in his district, stressing the need for more affordable and better quality health care. He followed that up by conducting a workshop on health care, held in February 1979 at Tennessee Tech University, in Cookeville, Tennessee. The workshop was a huge success and gave Gore the opportunity to inform his constituents on this issue. He proposed new initiatives designed to reduce the cost and increase the quality of health care, and continued to enhance his national popularity through the introduction of legislation dealing with health-care issues.[13] Gore also brought to the workshops professional speakers and experts in the health-care industry. Looking back, it is amazing that he was able to foresee the health-care crisis that we have today. If only more congressmen and senators had listened to him, maybe the health-care crisis would not have become as severe in later years.

It didn't take long for Al Gore to make a name for himself in the new Congress. He used his background as an investigative reporter to his advantage, focusing on the populist issues he campaigned on and that the people of the 4th District cared about. He was also extremely focused, exhibiting keen incite and political instincts from day one. But what no one knew at the time was just how fast

---

12 Kevin Ellis, Tennessean, 1987

13 US Congressman Al Gore Jr. Meeting, Announcement Letter, January 1979

he would succeed in Congress, on his long journey into national prominence. After he was sworn in as the new congressman from Tennessee, he was placed on the powerful Science and Technology Committee. This position gave Gore the opportunity to work on an array of cutting edge issues that were vitally important to both him and the American people. It would also provide him a forum for conducting more of the congressional hearings he was famous for, on such issues as consumer and environmental protection, health care, nuclear weapons, and Social Security. While on the Science and Technology Committee, Gore made a name for himself very quickly. In October of 1980, the *Washingtonian* magazine rated Gore as two of the more effective members of Congress, listing Gore as one of the most promising newcomers. He was praised by independent government watch groups for his ability to use his committee assignments to explore futuristic issues like genetics, organ transplants, medical research, environmental issues, and nuclear weapons strategic planning. Gore would zero in on these issues on his committees, hold hearings and investigations on these complex issues, before finally authoring and sponsoring legislative bills that would solve the problems. This was the pattern that Gore followed from day one in the House and is one he would continue to follow effectively later on in the United States Senate.[14]

In 1980, Gore authored and cosponsored the Infant Formula Act, which ensured that all infant formulas sold in the United States meet minimum nutrition and safety standards, while also requiring manufacturers to test and label the contents. The bill was passed by a wide margin in Congress and signed into law by President Jimmy Carter. Then later in 1981, Gore was the author and principal sponsor of legislation requiring the labeling of sodium content in processed foods, a bill that he gained support on from both the American Medical Association and the American Heart Association, in prompting Congress to take action. Gore commented on the impact of the legislation in one of his constituent letters. "This bill offers a new mechanism for effectively combating one of the major causes of high blood pressure. This affliction, which leads to heart

---

14 Al Gore for Senate Campaign Newsletter, 1984

disease, stroke, and kidney failure, can result from or be exacerbated by excessive intake of sodium. Health experts agree that most Americans consume daily amounts of sodium 10–20 times above safe and adequate levels. Moreover, large amounts of sodium are often present in foods we would never suspect."[15]As a result of Gore's bill, the Food and Drug administration established a voluntary labeling program within the food industry. Gore, once again, was the forerunner on an issue that, like so many others, would someday have a positive impact upon the nation and society. Gore was also at front and center on the environment, even before the 'keep the earth clean' campaign slogans became household phrases. In this effort he was one of the first members of Congress to probe into the dumping of hazardous waste and chemicals, and in 1980 he toured a neighborhood in Memphis that had a history of serious illnesses. There he discovered that the area had been exposed to the dumping of hazardous waste during the 1950s. A series of public hearings were held that same year, in Washington, as part of a national effort to clean up the environment. Later that year, Congressman Gore cosponsored the Superfund Act of 1980, which became the landmark legislation for environmental cleanup of hazardous waste, providing for industry-based fees on corporations that did not meet hazardous waste clean-up requirements.[16]

In 1983, Gore again investigated and uncovered another hazardous waste dump site in Almaville, Tennessee, in rural Rutherford County. He found that the site contained over 1,000 barrels of waste that contained solvents and materials deemed extremely hazardous and dangerous." He also released a landmark report by the Office of Technology Assessment (OTA), which made four principle suggestions for solving the threats from hazardous waste disposal."[17]Gore stated, "We hope to provide incentives for a dramatic decrease in the amount of waste generated, a dramatic increase in the amount recycled, and a decrease in the amount going into landfills." After the OTA report, Gore conducted congressional hearings in the House

---

15 Congressional Record, 1980 (Infant Formula Act)
16 Congressional Record, 1980 (Superfund Act)
17 Carolyn Shoulders, Tennessean, March 18, 1983

of Representatives and held public meetings on the issue of hazardous waste on the environment. There were many terrible things that Gore and his congressional Committee on Science and Technology discovered. One of the biggest discoveries was that large corporations were literally flooding our backyards, streams, and rivers with highly dangerous chemicals that would end up causing major healthcare issues, such as cancer and kidney disease. This would not only cause millions of deaths, but also increase the cost of health care for future generations.[18]

Another issue that was vitally important for the people was the oil crisis of the late seventies and early eighties, under both the Carter and Reagan administrations. Gore saw an open window on this issue and jumped in. As early as 1979, Gore was sending out letters to his constituents, warning them about the need to conserve energy, and the dangers of relying on OPEC for the majority of oil imported to the United States. Although Gore was pleased that his constituents were willing to cut back on the use of electricity in hopes of helping with the energy crisis, he was keenly aware that the powerful oil corporations were, at the same time, making billions of dollars of profits at the expense of the American taxpayer. Thus, it was with this mindset that he came out blasting about the hypocrisy that existed within the federal government in allowing the oil industry to run roughshod on the American people. So he directed much of his anger to the Reagan administration that took office in January 1981. It was nothing personal against President Reagan; after all, President Carter had served four years before with virtually the same federal regulators in the Justice Department. But it was the right time to advance the issue nationally.

Mobil Oil Corporation was in the process of taking over the smaller Marathon Oil. In this takeover, Gore immediately saw that it was nothing more than an attempt at price control, and he publicly cited the Reagan administration and Justice Department for allowing the corporate acquisition. Gore saw in this case a clear violation of the antitrust laws, which were written by Congress in the late 1800s to prevent monopolies and illegal corporate practices.

---

18 Carolyn Shoulders, Tennessean, November 18, 1983

Gore released a report from his House subcommittee that showed that "oil company acquisitions jumped from $532 million in 1978 to $12.2 billion in the first seven months of 1981." He attributed the increase in oil company acquisitions and mergers to a "hemorrhage of cash flow in an oil industry feeling secure in the green light sign" that less attention would be paid by the Reagan administration in enforcing the antitrust matters in the future."[19] Gore's pursuit against the big oil corporations would cause Congress to pass a "moratorium on oil company mergers and acquisitions for 12 to 18 months. Once again, it was Al Gore who was leading the way on an issue that to this day baffles the American people.

Gore also landed a seat on the House Select Committee on Intelligence. On this congressional committee, he was able to investigate and explore a wide range of issues that dealt with nuclear weapons and foreign policy. He would be briefed by the President's Cabinet with Top Secret information, which allowed him to gain even more knowledge about complex issues that were of importance to the United States. It was on this committee where Gore began an extensive educational process in the field of strategic nuclear weapons. For more than a year, he devoted eight hours a day studying courses developed by nuclear arms experts. That education would prove to be valuable not only for Gore but the nation as well. [20]

In 1982, Gore proposed a new strategic arms agreement between the United States and the Soviet Union. The plan called for eliminating the fear of a first strike by removing multiple warheads from US missiles and replacing them with single-warhead, mobile-based weapons. This concept was widely embraced by nuclear arms control experts in both political parties. It also gave Gore bargaining leverage with the Reagan administration.[21] In May 1983, Gore joined a handful of moderate Democrats in supporting President Reagan's MX Missile program. In exchange for his support, Gore lobbied the Reagan administration into reducing the nuclear arsenals of the United States and Soviet Union. The build-down scheme called for

19 Frank Gibson, Tennessean, December 15, 1981.
20 Tennessean News Report, August 18, 1982
21 Mike Shanahan, Tennessean, May 25, 1983

each superpower to scrap more nuclear weapons than it added to its arsenal each year. Gore and other key Democrats met privately with President Reagan and his national security staff to forge the bipartisan alliance. The compromise provided the foundation for future nuclear weapons reduction agreements with the Soviet Union, while also providing Gore with another major accomplishment to his ever growing resume. Gore shared his thoughts about the nuclear arms race in an article in *The New Republic* in May 1982.[22]

"Before we can reach a meaningful arms control agreement with the Soviet Union, we must first reach an agreement among ourselves about what we are seeking. The time has come for the country as a whole to settle on some priorities in arms control—and to pursue them with as much single-mindedness as we can muster. We must make nuclear war less likely, not more likely. If the administration chooses wisely at this fork in the road, we will have a better opportunity to create a relationship with the Soviet Union which deters aggression—and which condemns war as 'an old habit of thought that must now pass.'"[23]

Congressman Gore tackled another public problem and nightmare: Social Security. Gore, along with Congressman Claude Pepper, of Florida, conducted a series of public meetings on the issue of Social Security and the need to transform the system before it went bankrupt. He also conducted special open meetings throughout the 4th District, trying to gain ideas from the people on the best way to fix the Social Security problem both now and in the future. Along these lines, Gore worked with Congressman Pepper to help bridge the gap on Medicare and the illegal practices of insurance providers, and co-authored, with Pepper, a bill that helped increase senior citizens' awareness of fraudulent insurance practices. Gore also worked with Congressman Pepper on Alzheimer's disease, calling attention to the need for more research and education to try to help identify and prevent its causes, while also providing for funding from the federal government for research and outpatient services.[24]

---

22 Albert Gore Jr., "The Fork in the Road," The New Republic, May 5, 1982, 13-16
23 Ibid.
24 US Congressman Al Gore Jr., Meeting Announcement Letter, January 1983

Al Gore was a tireless campaigner, who approached seeking votes like he did everything else—full speed ahead. His physical presence was commanding and authoritative, with his blue suit and red tie making him look important and larger than life. But he also put people at ease with his friendly demeanor and occasional folksy talk, with an occasional "yall" or "howdy". When he would make a speech, he would always use good grammar and formally address his audience. However, when he held a meeting in the rural areas of the district, he would use language that was more down to earth than the language he would use if he were addressing the Murfreesboro Chamber of Commerce. But he was always consistent in his approach to meeting people and working a room; he would try to shake hands with everyone and, in most instances, he didn't have to go to them. They came to him in droves and lined up to meet him and talk to him about their personal problems or to simply exchange greetings. Looking back, I am amazed at how many meetings he conducted, and how many people that he personally helped. Even back then, Gore was extremely focused, disciplined, and driven. Another important tool for keeping in touch with his old friends and constituents was the annual Gore family Christmas card, with Al, Tipper, and family appearing on the front of the card. His congressional office staff would send out thousands of these full-color cards every year at the first of December. If you didn't get a Christmas card from him, then it meant either you were not on his list of supporters, or the mailman just made an error. In any case it was really a big deal to receive the annual Gore Christmas card. It was another way to stay in touch with the people, something the founding fathers would have approved of most assuredly.

In 1984, Congress passed one of Gore's greatest legislative accomplishments, the National Organ Transplant Act. Gore authored and sponsored the bill in the House, along with Senator Orin Hatch (R-Utah) in the Senate, which called for the establishment of a nationwide organ donor network linking organ donors with transplant patients in an efficient manner. It also required for an annual review of transplant operations to ensure that coverage guidelines and procedures were properly enforced by private insurers and hospitals. In addition, the bill made it unlawful for anyone to buy or sell body organs. President Reagan initially opposed this legislation but ultimately agreed to sign the bill. The act was signed by Reagan and went into law in October 1984.[25]

The Tennessee congressman shared his views on this bill during an October 1983 interview with the *Tennessean*. "We are in a new era of organ transplants and the demand is going to grow more rapidly than the supply," Gore said. "It is essential for us to establish a national strategy for organ transplantation. There are 20,000 brain deaths annually and that tragedy is compounded by the fact that only 2,200 cases result in organ donation. Attitudes are changing, but we must do more."[26] In each of these populist issues, Gore effectively used his communication skills in swaying public opinion in support of his legislation. Before introducing the organ transplant bill, Gore held a series of congressional hearings with physicians and health-care experts. The bill was delayed in the House Ways and Means Committee because of opposition to Medicare involvement, along with disagreement on how the transplant centers would be chosen. President Reagan also initially opposed the legislation, citing the need to keep organ transplantation in the private sector, coordinated by voluntary groups. This conservative approach to a national issue that required government intervention was disturbing to Gore, so he continued to press the president and his administration on the issue. Finally, after months of debate, the administration finally conceded to the Gore–Waxman bill, with President Reagan signing the legislation into law in October 1984. Gore commented on the administration's decision shortly after Reagan signed the bill. "Almost eighty-percent of Americans are willing to donate organs, but they are not asked. This new national system will make it much easier to obtain lifesaving organs for transplantation. We believe it can triple the rate of organ donation. I'm pleased that President Reagan has signed the legislation."[27] This was another major legislative achievement for Congressman Gore, and another example of how Gore used his political and investigative skills in identifying a

---

25 Congressional Record, October 1984 (National Organ Transplant Act)

26 Adel Crowe, Tennessean, October 5, 1984

27 Ibid.

complex, problematic issue and conducting congressional hearings on the subject before finally negotiating with the president and Congress in getting the bill passed into law.

Sometimes Gore could show an intense anger. On one occasion, in the late 1970s, just after he was elected to Congress, he encountered a supporter who walked up to him and proceeded to tell him about all the hard work he had done for him during his congressional campaign in 1976. Gore immediately recognized the man, but recalled that the man was not one of his original campaign supporters and, instead, had worked for his opponent in the race. But Gore played along anyway and shook hands with the man and thanked him. Then, a few minutes after the man had left, Gore, with fire in his eyes and redness across his face, turned to one of his longtime campaign chairmen and said, "Does he think I'm a damn fool?"

By the end of his fourth term in the House, Gore had established himself as one of the most effective congressmen in either political party. He was consistently rated as one of the top ten congressmen by independent congressional watch groups, and one year a Washington-based magazine that followed Congress ranked Gore as the sixth top member of the entire Congress. Thus, out of 435 members of Congress, Al Gore was at the top. This did not surprise any of his family, friends, and supporters. It was yet another example which demonstrated Al Gore was truly a politician for the people, one who had gone to Washington to fight for and defend his constituents on any issue he felt caused conflict with the people. In short, he was living up to being what the founding fathers conceived in the Constitution—a representative and voice for the people.

Al Gore also maintained an attendance voting record of 99.6 percent, another high mark for the congressman from Tennessee, and became popular with consumer advocacy groups for his unrelenting work in helping people with such issues as affordable health care, environmental protection, or social security reform, to name a few. *The Almanac of American Politics* said that Gore "has compiled a thoughtful record not only on issues before his committees but also on such distant matters as arms control. Gore at age 35, seems to have all the qualifications to be a Senator and important leader for the National Democratic Party too." One independent group,

Politics in America, said of Gore, "Few in Congress can match his ability to seize an issue, uncover a pattern of abuses, draw attention in the media and propose a solution."[28] That assessment summed up Gore's great ability and talent as a congressman and statesman. Indeed Congressman Al Gore had gained a good reputation and national following for his hard work on very complex and important issues of concern to the nation. He demonstrated an insatiable appetite in making a positive difference on the nation and world, and it would only be a matter of time before Gore would become an even more influential national political leader.

---

28 Politics in America, 1984, Congressional Quarterly Press

CHAPTER 4

United States Senate Campaign

After nearly four terms in the House of Representatives, Congressman Al Gore had become one of the rising stars of the Democratic Party. Thus it was not surprising that his eyes were on the bigger prize, the United States Senate. The only obstacle was that the two US Senate seats in Tennessee were already taken. Senator Jim Sasser, the Democratic senator from Nashville, had been elected senator the same year that Gore was elected to the House of Representatives in 1976. The other US senate seat was held by Senator Howard Baker (R-Huntsville), who had been elected in 1966, and had gained national fame on the Nixon Watergate Committee as vice-chairman of the senate hearings. Senator Baker had been a Republican presidential candidate in 1976 and 1980, and was a very popular moderate Republican senator. The people in Tennessee loved Senator Baker, and there was no indication that he was ready to step down. Thus it came as a complete surprise when Senator Baker suddenly announced, in the fall of 1983, that he would not seek re-election to the US Senate. With that announcement, Congressman

Albert Gore Jr. became the odds-on favorite to succeed Senator Baker. Gore could not have been more prepared and ready for the moment, and the opportunity to ascend to the next political level was finally at hand.

Gore had built up such a formidable political base throughout the 4th and 6th Districts, and throughout the state of Tennessee, that it was virtually certain he would become the Democratic nominee for the US Senate. He had served over seven years in Congress, with distinction, and built a reputation for being one of the best and brightest in all of Congress, and now his time had finally come. The only question seemed to be who the Republicans would choose to run against him. Gore made his official campaign announcement in his hometown of Carthage, Tennessee, on the steps of the old courthouse, with hundreds of supporters, friends, and family on hand. Tipper and Gore's mother and father looked on with delight, as they were witnessing another Gore statewide campaign, but this time for Al Gore Jr., whose day had finally arrived. It was now time to wage another Gore political campaign.

The Republican Party in Tennessee would have a very difficult time finding a candidate that could compete with the popular congressman from Carthage. Looking around the state, there did not appear to be anyone in the Republican Party that could come close to matching Gore's popularity, and there would likely be a fight for the GOP nomination. Nevertheless, there would finally be one candidate who would emerge as the front-runner for the Republicans— Senator Victor Ashe, from Knoxville. Ashe had spent sixteen years in the General Assembly of Tennessee and had gained a reputation as a maverick politician. He was regarded as a bright young man who had the talent to propose complex legislation but who sometimes lacked the political skills to get the legislation passed. While Ashe was very popular in Knoxville and East Tennessee and had the key Republican contacts necessary to gain the Republican nomination, he was virtually unknown across of the rest of the state. Gore, on the other hand, could count on high name recognition throughout the entire state, and thus it would undoubtedly be an uphill battle for Ashe and the Republican Party against Gore, with his impressive political campaign machine.

Quickly all political eyes in Tennessee and the nation turned to the senate race between Gore and Ashe. Both campaigns prepared to face each other, since all polling showed that both candidates were their party's favorites to win their respective nomination. In addition to Gore and Ashe, there was an Independent candidate named Ed McAteer from Memphis, Tennessee, who put his name in the race. McAteer was the executive director of a conservative evangelical group located in Memphis. The issues he talked most about were lower taxes, abortion, and big government. But McAteer's candidacy would help Gore more than hurt him, because as conservative and evangelical, McAteer's followers generally voted Republican. Thus, a vote for McAteer generally ended up taking one away from Ashe, and ultimately this created a big problem that Ashe could never overcome.

Congressman Gore was also helped by the entire Tennessee Democratic Party establishment. Unlike in the past, when there were always factions within the state Democratic Party, the party had been united since 1976. Gore could also rely on US Senator Jim Sasser (D-Nashville) and the younger wing of the Democratic Party to support his candidacy. His efforts were also boosted by the fact that he currently represented the 6th Congressional District, which he had taken over in 1982 after the Tennessee legislature gerrymandered the state's congressional districts. Since Gore was from Carthage, in the upper part of North Central Tennessee near the Kentucky border, it made sense to give Gore a different district, one that would allow him to become better known in other counties within the state while also allowing the Democrats to gain an additional seat in Gore's old 4th Congressional District. The net affect was that Gore had already represented almost one-third of all the counties in Tennessee, which was another major advantage that he had over candidates that might oppose him in his bid for the Senate.

Early on in the campaign, it became evident that Victor Ashe would try to paint Gore as a big-spending liberal who was out of touch with the average Tennessean. In so doing, he seemed to be borrowing from the playbook of Bill Brock, a former senator who used the same argument in his campaign against Gore's father in the bitter 1970 Senate campaign. The only problem was that Gore was far from being liberal, and he was very much in touch with the people of Tennessee. Gore would counter with his leadership ability and success in passing important national legislation. "I have defined the central issue in this campaign to be effectiveness," Gore said. "The Comprehensive Crime Control Act and the Organ Transplant bill serve as evidence that I can get things done in the United States Congress." In an interview during the campaign, Gore also defended his record of public service. "The old labels—liberal and conservative—have far less relevance to today's problems than the efforts to find solutions to those problems. There's no need to rely on an outdated ideology as a crutch. The judgment of my constituents in four trips to the ballot box is far better evidence than the charge of a political opponent,"[29] said Gore.

The Gore campaign quickly organized a political organization that was the envy of every politician who had ever run for statewide office in Tennessee. By midsummer of 1984, the Gore campaign had raised nearly $1.8 million in campaign contributions. Most of the campaign contributions were less than $200 each, but he also managed to rake in a large number of contributions ranging from $500 to $1000. The Gore campaign used another ingenious tactic to gain even more campaign funds from the average Tennessean. On March 24, 1984, Gore sent out a mass letter to his friends and supporters across the state, announcing that he would have a statewide "Get Together for Gore" on May 31, 1984. This event would involve hundreds of "Get Togethers" in private homes, hosted simultaneously by Gore's key supporters across the state in all ninety-five counties. The event would feature Gore in a special television program, where he would announce his candidacy, outline the keys to his campaign, and ask for volunteers to help in his bid for the Senate. The events were designed to bring in between $200 and $250 in small contributions of $10 to $20 each. These small contributions helped the campaign to broaden its financial base throughout the state. It also allowed new supporters to sign up to become a campaign volunteer.[30]

Gore also gained financial support from many contributors within the national Democratic Party and from friends and support-

---

29 Ed Cromer, Tennessean, June 17, 1984

30 Gore US Senate Campaign Newsletter, March 1984

ers in other states. For example, a private fund-raising event was held in Nashville, Tennessee, on May 21, 1983, at a supporter's home in Belle Meade, with tickets costing $500 per couple. Then later that night, Gore joined several hundred more supporters near downtown Nashville. Walter Mondale, the former vice president, was in attendance, along with Senator Fritz Hollings of South Carolina, both of whom were running for president in 1984. The events were very successful, with Gore raking in several hundred thousand dollars. The campaign events and small fundraisers proved to be an overwhelming success and helped solidify Gore's lead over Victor Ashe in the state polls. By the beginning of summer, polling conducted across the state showed Al Gore with almost a 2 to 1 lead over Victor Ashe. This reaffirmed Gore's popularity throughout the state, and meant that Al was running an effective campaign.

Al Gore was a natural campaigner, and when he would meet voters in person, he would use his charm to grab their attention. He had that rare ability to connect with people, making them feel as if they were the most important person in the world. He was known to go out of his way trying to land that last vote, no matter how difficult it might be. One day, while campaigning in rural West Tennessee, Gore made a campaign stop where there were several farmers gathered. He jumped out of the car and briskly walked up to the group of farmers and said, "Hi, I'm Al Gore, and your name?" He managed to shake every hand and talk to every single farmer there. Gore pursued each person for a handshake as though the failure to shake a hand might be the one vote that cost him the election. As he would leave one person to shake the hand of another, he used the closing statement, "I need your help. Have a good day."[31]

Ashe did continue to go on the attack against Gore, calling him out for voting for tax increases and supporting big government, while trying to make the Senate race a referendum on President Ronald Reagan. Ashe knew the only way to beat Gore would be to show he was the more conservative candidate and try to ride President Reagan's coattails into the Senate. Reagan was extremely popular in Tennessee, like he was in most of the country. That strategy was

---

31 Jim O'Hara, Tennessean, October 7, 1984.

flawed, however, because every time Ashe tried to show he was more conservative, like Reagan, Gore would turn around and say that he had personally worked with the president on many issues, and that he supported him on national defense issues, like the MX Missile; he would also say that party labels, like liberal and conservative, did not apply to him, because he sometimes voted with Reagan on issues. He described himself as a moderate, and was able to demonstrate that fact by outlining issues he had supported that were both conservative and liberal. Nevertheless, Gore also went out of his way to distance himself from the presidential race, telling voters that the presidential and Senate campaigns were two separate races. He did point out, however, that there were some issues where he disagreed with Vice President Walter Mondale, Reagan's Democratic opponent.

By June of 1984, Congressman Gore began amassing an impressive number of newspaper endorsements across the state of Tennessee. He was endorsed by the *Tennessean*, a traditionally Democratic leaning newspaper located in Nashville, but also by its rival, the *Nashville Banner*, a conservative, Republican-leaning newspaper. Gore also picked up endorsements from the *Memphis Commercial Appeal* and *Jackson Sun* newspapers, both West Tennessee publications, and gathered endorsements from the majority of the smaller newspapers across Middle Tennessee, in the counties that he represented in Congress. He even managed to win several newspaper endorsements from the Republican stronghold of East Tennessee, including Morristown, Elizabethton, and Knoxville. In endorsing Gore, the *Rutherford Courier* said, "He works with the administration when he truly feels the administration's approach is the right path. But when he feels the administration is not acting in our best interest, he offers constructive alternatives, many of which are heeded." The *Elizabethton Star* described Gore as "the candidate who has proven time and time again that he is the man for the job," and said, "We heartily endorse his candidacy, Democrats, and Independents, alike, in Washington and on the national front."[32] Among the powerful special interest groups, Gore picked up the endorsements of the Teachers, the Veterans of Foreign Wars (VFW); the Teamsters; the

---

32 Gore US Senate Campaign Newsletter, June 1984

Police and Firefighters; and even some of the conservative business groups. The campaign could not seem to do anything wrong, and Gore's prospects looked brighter each day.

However, there would be one tragic moment during the 1984 campaign that would shake Gore, leaving him in deep emotional pain. His beloved sister, Nancy Gore Hungar, died of cancer after a long battle with the disease. Nancy's death was devastating to Al and his family. It would prove to be the biggest emotional moment of his life. He looked up to Nancy, and she had always been his supporter, mediator, adviser, and loving critic. Losing her really shook Al, and he would carry the emotional pain for a very long time. Later, he would describe this difficult time: "Nancy was beautiful, vibrant, and strong. But lung cancer proved too cruel an adversary. I was in the midst of my first campaign for the US Senate, when my father called and said Nancy was fading. I rushed to her bedside. My mother and father were there in the room, along with Tipper, and of course Frank Hunger, Nancy's beloved husband. I looked into her eyes and said I love you, Nancy. I knelt by the bed holding her hand for a long time and soon she took her last breath and slipped away."[33]

As the campaign moved forward, Gore managed to catch his breath again. He then went back into full swing, making campaign stops across the state of Tennessee. He went into the rural areas, the small towns, and the large cities. In all, the candidate would visit all 95 counties in the state, meeting with farmers, laborers, teachers, bankers, and lawyers, never seeming to run out of hands to shake or stops to make. It was vintage Al Gore.

There would be a series of campaign debates between Gore, Ashe, and McAteer, with the first debate held on September 16, 1984. In the first debate, Gore was confident and energized and didn't hesitate in attacking his opponents. He immediately charged into Victor Ashe, putting him on the defensive while stating facts about Ashe's record in the state Senate. This seemed to catch Ashe off guard, and so he spent the rest of the night playing defence. Gore also scored points on style and theme, and delivered substantive answers to the

---

33 Al Gore, An Inconvient Truth, 2006

questions that were asked by the moderator. It was a very tough night for Victor Ashe.

Gore was a great debater, having learned many of his skills from his days at Harvard. He was a natural at putting his opponents on the defensive with a series of quotes about his record, and when his opponents would try to turn the tables on him, Gore always seemed to be able to turn the attack back in the face of his attacker. He would throw out stats and quotes like an IBM computer, never seeming to miss a beat. The advantage he had during his debate performances was often so lopsided that the viewers got the feeling they were watching a boxing match, wondering when they would see real blood flow onto the stage. During one of the debates, Ashe brought up the charge that Tennesseans were conservative, like President Reagan, and wanted someone who would vote that way with the president. Gore retorted back in classic style, stating that "one of my opponents will likely try to confuse you into thinking this race is nothing more than an extension of the presidential race. That Tennessee doesn't need a Senator of its own, who will respond to you and fight for you, that it can make do with a coattail or a rubber stamp."[34] It was another knockdown punch for Gore, and Ashe could barely get back up. But the debate performances were not a coincidence. They were well planned, as Gore would spend hours rehearsing for his upcoming debates, and many more hours reading over his opponent's record on issues that might have seemed remote to the average person. His hard work paid big dividends when he went to the stage. After the first debate, Victor Ashe seemed to be off key during the remaining debates, and could never get back on track. While he would continue to attack Al's record and call him a big liberal spender, Gore would simply recall all of his many accomplishments in passing meaningful legislation that had a positive and measurable impact upon society. He would also remind Ashe that he went along with many of President Reagan's agenda items, and recalled his support of the MX Missile program as an example. Gore said that he supported the Reagan administration when he thought they were doing things right, and debated them on issues, such as the oil industry to big corporations, when he thought the direction they were headed was not in the

---

34 Carol Bradley, Nashville Banner, September 17, 1984

best interests of the people. Then Gore would attack Ashe's record, or lack thereof in most cases. After the first debate, with Gore not making any mistakes, he could now run out the clock in the remaining public debates. The race was Gore's for the taking and he knew it, as did everyone else, even the most ardent Republicans. It was only a question of how large the margin of victory would be.

On Election Day, Gore voted early in his hometown of Carthage, Tennessee. As he left the polling precinct, he smiled and shook hands before getting in his car and heading back to his campaign headquarters in downtown Nashville, a short distance away. He would spend much of his day at his headquarters, before finally arriving at the Vanderbilt Plaza Hotel, his election night campaign headquarters. He went up to his Hotel Suite and relaxed for a few hours, making several phone calls to key supporters and campaign operatives across the state. The early exit polling was looking good, and Gore's campaign staff predicted in private that he would win in a landslide.

On election night, Gore and his family and campaign staff watched the early voting results in his suite. Meanwhile, downstairs, thousands of loud and raucous Gore friends and supporters were gathered watching and waiting. On the television monitors, the vote totals trickled in, with Gore surging to a big lead. At one point Gore was winning by almost 70 percent of the vote, and was leading in all areas of the state. It was now clear that Congressman Gore would win the race in an overwhelming fashion. At approximately 8:30 p.m. (CST), Gore took to the stage and told his screaming supporters, "You have responded with a vote so overwhelming as to assume historic proportions and I thank you. I fully realize the state is losing a great deal with Howard Baker leaving."[35] He also said that he had scheduled a meeting with Governor Lamar Alexander (R-Maryville) the next day, in order to start an immediate transition. Gore had amassed 990,909 votes; Victor Ashe had garnered 553,202 votes, and Ed McAteer had come in third with 85,710 votes. Gore won all nine of the Tennessee congressional districts, as well as eighty-three of the state's ninety-five counties, even beating Victor Ashe in his home county (Knox). Ashe, meanwhile, managed to win only twelve counties, all of which

35 Carol Bradley and Bruce Dobie, *Nashville Banner*, November 5, 1984

were in Republican-dominated East Tennessee. Gore managed to win over seventeen counties in East Tennessee, something that no other Democrat had done since Reconstruction, with his vote totals also breaking the record as the largest total of votes in Tennessee history. This showed just how popular and effective Gore was as a campaigner and legislator. Indeed it was an impressive number of votes that Gore had racked up, and it reaffirmed his popularity throughout Tennessee. President Reagan defeated Walter Mondale by a count of 989,868 to 697,800 votes, almost the identical total that Gore had amassed. The bad news for Victor Ashe was that there were no Reagan coattails to ride, and the only tails in the election were the ones that got kicked by Al Gore.

In keeping with their reputation, Tennessee voters once again showed the desire to elect moderate politicians, regardless of the political party affiliation. In Al Gore, they saw someone they could trust who would work hard in representing them in Washington. Even Gore's opponents had to admit that he was an amazing politician, and soon everyone across the state and nation began to realize it too. The day after the election, Senator-elect Gore met with Governor Lamar Alexander at the governor's mansion in Nashville to begin the transition process, as he had planned. He told the governor that he intended to carry on Senator Howard Baker's tradition of non-partisanship in his efforts to fight and work for the good of the people of Tennessee. The men had a very cordial meeting, and even though they had opposing political ideologies, they respected each other and realized they needed to work together on many issues that were critical to the state of Tennessee. Senator Gore also pledged that he would be a senator for all the people and would work with President Reagan as necessary to address issues that were vital to Tennessee and its people. Now it was time for Gore to turn his attention to that gentleman's club known as the United States Senate, and he could not have been happier. At only thirty-six, Gore was one of the youngest senators elected in Tennessee history. He was overjoyed to be restoring the Gore name in the Senate, where his father had served for eighteen years. Indeed it was a very happy day for the Gore family and for his many friends and campaign supporters. However this would only be one more step along the way to Al Gore's political future.

CHAPTER 5

The Senate Years: 1985–1993

Before becoming the new senator from Tennessee, Al Gore was widely seen as someone to watch for in the future. He set up his offices in the Hart Senate office building in Washington D.C., residing in the same room that former Presidents John F. Kennedy and Richard Nixon had both occupied when they were US Senators. He also assembled a top notch Senate staff and established district offices throughout Tennessee, ensuring that his constituents had access to him and his staff at all times.

Now that he had taken a step forward in his political journey and won a seat in the Senate, Gore felt it was vitally important to be assigned to a major committee, where he could use his talent and skills to continue advancing his populist ideas and political career. After he was sworn in as senator, Gore was placed on the Committee on Governmental Affairs in the United States Senate. He was also appointed to the Senate's Commerce and Rules Committee. The Commerce Committee allowed Senator Gore the opportunity to focus on many of the consumer and health-care causes that he had

championed while in the House of Representatives. Though he was
placed on important committees, he ranked near the bottom of the
Senate in seniority. His low ranking, however, did not deter him;
he instead viewed it as an opportunity: "I'm happy to be 96th in
seniority instead of 100th. And I'm happy simply to be here." He
also shared his ideas on what he hoped to accomplish as a member
of the US Senate: "I hope to develop a bipartisan plan to reduce the
budget deficit, and I hope to help gain a verifiable and meaningful
arms control agreement with the Soviet Union."[36]

Al Gore's career in the US Senate would prove to be a resounding success. He continued to champion populist issues and fight
for the people against corporate and governmental barriers, and
also continued to be a strong proponent of national defense issues,
voting for most of the major military contracts that the Pentagon
requested. His schedule in the Senate was very hectic. On a typical day he would work twelve to sixteen hours, attending briefings,
meetings, and media interviews. Gore was very popular by now,
and he was in big demand by the national media. Everyone from
the *Los Angeles Times* and *Washington Post* to various television sta-
tions wanted time from the senator. He also would meet with constituents and lobbyists in Washington, always seeming to find time
for that last constituent who was either seeking a job or needing
help with a federal agency. In addition to his exhaustive schedule in
his Washington office, Senator Gore would continue to hold open
town hall meetings with his constituents throughout all ninety-
five counties in Tennessee. He would fly in on weekends, traveling
through five counties at a time, in keeping with his schedule. This
was designed to allow him to visit constituents in all of the state's
ninety-five counties by the end of each year. Moreover, he would
spend part of his summer vacation conducting many of the open
meetings he had scheduled. He would benefit from the open meetings by listening to his constituents, as they often gave him ideas
on issues that needed to be addressed in Washington. On a typical
open meeting day, Gore would begin by providing the people with
an update on the current issues in Washington affecting them. Then

36 Pat Daly, *Tennessean*, Jan. 27, 1985.

he would answer questions from everyone who held up a hand, always aware that every word he said would be taped by the media. After taking questions for an hour, sometimes an hour and a half, he would then dismiss the meeting. Next he would walk to the back of the room where he would then shake hands with everyone as they left the room. He also would sometimes talk one-on-one with constituents about their private matters, whether it was problems with Social Security, Medicare, Veterans Affairs, or soliciting a job. Gore would write down their concerns and hand them over to his staff, who in turn would then take the concerns back to the local Senate district office and go to work trying to help solve the issue. And in every county that he went to for an open meeting, you could be sure the local newspaper or radio station would have a representative on hand. Gore would field their questions, and in turn they would usually publish an article on the front page of their newspaper. This went on every year while Al Gore was in Congress, a total of sixteen years of meeting with his constituents, all the while maintaining a 98.6 percent voting record in Congress. It is utterly amazing to look back now and see how much time and work he did for the people. There was no slowing down the pace that he had set, and he never seemed to run out of energy. Upon reflection, it is equally amazing that, despite his hectic work schedule, Gore still managed to spend lots of time with his four children.

Gore was a moderate Democrat who supported President Ronald Reagan on many issues, but when he disagreed with the president, he was not shy about letting it be known. In June of 1985, Senator Gore applauded President Reagan's decision to proceed with the SALT II disarmament agreement with the Soviet Union. Reagan's decision to move forward with SALT II meant that he would try to work with the Soviets in reducing nuclear weapons and improving relations. Senator Gore stated that "For many months now I have argued that we should comply in both principle and fact with the agreement." "It has given us the only anchor for US-Soviet relations during a stormy period." "This decision, which underscores the president's commitment to reaching an arms control agreement during his term, puts pressure on the Soviets to respond to our offers of a verifiable accord in Geneva." Gore was also chosen as one of ten US Senators to monitor the progress of peace talks with the Russians at the Geneva Peace Accord in 1985.[37]

Gore impressed the arms control community not only with his intellect, but also with his ability to focus on an issue and make headlines. James P. Rubin, an arms control expert with the Arms Control Association, summed up Gore's ability in an interview: "Yes he does want to be on the news. But the reason people like me take him seriously is the way he chooses his issues and what he chooses to make news about." James Woolsey, a key US arms negotiator, said Gore was "one of the very few members of Congress who has been a genuine intellectual contributor to the debate."[38]

During Al Gore's first term in the US Senate, in 1986 the Senate took a giant leap in changing the way they conducted business. In a bill that was cosponsored by Senator Gore, the US Senate passed legislation that allowed live television coverage of the Senate proceedings (the resolution passed the Senate by a vote of 67–21). This was a very big deal, for the US Senate had always been sort of a gentleman's club that kept its quarters closed as much as allowed by law, which meant very little access. Prior to this, the only way the people could see their senators at work was to attend the live proceedings in the Senate Chamber. Now the US Senate proceedings could be viewed via live television and radio. This ushered in a new era of more open government, and was seen as a real plus for the nation. Senator Gore later stated that: "Putting the Senate on the airwaves will give the American people an opportunity not only to hear government in action, but to take part in it. Now that the Americans will be listening to the Senate, every Senator will take special care to listen to them. Televising the Senate will be a great stride toward making democracy work," Gore stated.[39]

Also in the same year, Senator Gore introduced the Supercomputer Network Study Act of 1986, which was designed to advance computer technology throughout the government and industry. Senator Gore was particularly interested in seeing the computer technology used to

---

37 Mike Pigott, *Nashville Banner*, June 11, 1985.
38 Ibid.
39 Article by Senator Albert Gore Jr., 1986.

increase and enhance the sharing of information throughout society. Moreover, he saw the potential of the technology and how it could have a profound impact upon our world. He referred to the technology as the "information superhighway," later known as the Internet. Then later on in the Senate, Gore authored the High Performance Computing and Communication Act of 1991, commonly referred to as the Gore Bill. The bill was passed into law on December 9, 1991, and led to the National Information Infrastructure Act, which Gore co-authored in the Senate. Later on in his career Senator Gore would receive criticism from his political opponents on the Internet issue for statements that he made to a reporter. Gore stated that he "took the initiative in creating the internet", referring to his initiatives in Congress, where he was one of the first politicians to talk about and advance the concept of the information superhighway, and was one of the authors of national legislation that laid the framework for what we now know as the Internet. Even Newt Gingrinch, the former Republican House Speaker defended Gore on this issue. In a speech before the National Political Science Association in 2000, Gingrinch said "in all fairness it's something (internet) that Gore had worked on a long time". "Gore is the person, who in Congress most systematically worked to make sure that we got to an internet". Indeed, Al Gore played an important role in the advancement of computer technology in our society, but has received little credit for his efforts.

In 1987, Senator Gore was assigned to the powerful Senate Armed Services Committee. This was a major turning point for Gore's career. While in the House of Representatives, Gore had impressed both the Democrats and Republicans in his mastery of the complex issue of nuclear weapons reduction, thus it was natural that the Democrats in the Senate would appoint Gore to this particular committee. The Armed Services Committee would allow Gore to focus his attention on defense and national security issues, like nuclear arms control and military funding, and Gore would use this position to further his career while also providing expertise to the nation on its military and national affairs. In the process he was also receiving national attention from members of Congress and Democratic Party officials, with his name frequently mentioned as a potential presidential candidate. Gore continued to make more headlines as a member of the Senate subcommittee assigned to investigate NASA in the aftermath of the space shuttle *Challenger* disaster, and he would once again demonstrate his investigative skills. During the questioning of NASA officials, Gore uncovered some horrifying facts about the agency and its safety guidelines, with the officials admitting that NASA had cut its quality control personnel by almost 70 percent after the moon landing. Gore and the other subcommittee members were stunned and outraged, and as a result launched more hearings. After the hearings, NASA focused more on safety and quality assurance; two areas found lacking both before and after the *Challenger* tragedy. Gore's subcommittee had a profound effect upon how NASA would conduct quality control testing in the future and most likely saved the agency from other disasters in the future.

Gore always looked out for the working class and poor, time and time again. If he saw the slightest evidence of corporations trying to bully the people, he would go after them like a bulldog, relentless in his pursuit to correct the wrongs and bring justice to the people through passage of legislation that protected them from the evils that be. It was not that he was anti-business; it was just that most of the time he found that the big corporations could not be trusted to do what was right for the working people.

"You two keep in touch with and let me know what's going on," said the Senator from Carthage. I replied, "You don't have to worry about us." Then Jess O'Dear, Gore's Franklin County Chairman, and I said goodbye to him and left. It was 1986, and Al Gore had just completed another one of his town hall meetings. He was tired as he left us and headed toward the waiting car. But he always took time to check on how his local campaign was doing, never taking anything for granted. Jess had been one of Gore's county chairmen from the beginning, and Jess's mother, Aunt Lucy O'Dear, had campaigned hard for Al Gore Sr. when he was a congressman and senator, going door to door talking to voters, and, more importantly, using her family's influence to gain votes for him. That's the way politicking was done in the days before television, and it was the only way for a political candidate to win large numbers of voters.

In 1987, Tipper Gore wrote and published her book *"Raising PG Kids in an X-Rated Society"*. Tipper had been persuaded to take public action on the subject of inappropriate lyrics and content in records and videos, after discovering that one of the Gore's daughters had obtained a record with explicit lyrics. Tipper was determined to make a difference in society, and she followed through. Her book was received with high praise from families and religious organizations, but was met with disdain and disgust by the entertainment and recording industry. However, Tipper was undeterred by her critics, and testified before Congress calling for 'voluntary labeling' of records and videos throughout the recording industry. After several years of debate, the industry finally relented to content labeling. Her fight for family values would prove to be an asset for society and for her husband Al Gore, as it demonstrated that their family was willing to take a stand for what was right, regardless of political party affiliation or ideology.

While Al Gore had worked well with the Reagan administration on many issues, he would face more difficulty working with President George H. W. Bush. It was not that Gore had changed his political ideology; it was more like the new administration was more difficult to negotiate and compromise with. Gore even let it be known on the floor of the Senate that he was much more comfortable with Ronald Reagan than George Bush. "[Reagan] was predictable. You knew where he was coming from and where he was going. With George Bush you do not know either, and he does not know himself."[40]

Senator Gore would take on the Bush administration many times, and there was no shortage of chances. On one such occasion, Vice President Dan Quayle was quoted as saying that President Reagan's call for a Star Wars system designed to protect the United States from incoming nuclear weapons was a "pipe dream," while trying to sell a newer version of the defense system called the "Strategic Defense Initiative (SDI)." Gore pounced on this like a cat on a mouse, stating that, "It's the morning after in America." They're facing a new budget situation. I don't think Bush can keep a straight

---

40 Congressional Record, April 8, 1992.

face and pull off the same routine Reagan pulled off for so many years." He called the Bush administration's actions "the old bait and switch routine" and said "They sell an illusion, get the customer into the store and switch to another model." Gore also lamented the Bush administration spending $17 billion for the SDI, but he would eventually support the SDI, later named the Missile Defense System, a ground-based missile shield designed to seek and destroy incoming missiles in the air before they reached US territory. Gore would prove to be a strong supporter of both the Missile Defense System and other military defense projects during his Senate career, adding to his resume a reputation as a moderate Democrat who was strong on National Defense and Military issues.[41]

While in the Senate, Gore also focused on the environment, as he had done as a Congressman, and his reputation as an environmentalist became even more widely known. In 1990, he introduced a bill called the World Environment Policy Act and won passage of the resolution in Congress that called for an international agreement on Antarctica, which, among other things, halted mining and drilling on the continent. The continent of Antarctica was of particular concern and interest to the Senator because of its unique relationship to the earth's environment, and he was convinced that the earth's ozone layer was becoming depleted by rising temperatures, which were the result of an increase in carbon dioxide. Moreover, he used that argument to help gain passage of legislation in Congress that was designed to protect the continent. "We have a rare opportunity to protect a pristine environment dangerously at risk from development. We can act now for this generation and generations to come; or we can legislate and lose an irreplaceable resource," the Senator stated.[42] He also supported efforts to pass the International Plan to Protect the Stratospheric Ozone Layer, a bill that President George Bush opposed. In the same year, Gore headed the Senate delegation to the Rio de Janeiro summit. While at the Summit, he challenged the Bush administration on global warming, and was critical of President Bush for not agreeing to sign the treaty on climate

---

41 Germond and Witcover Article, 1991.
42 Patrick Willard, *Nashville Banner,* Oct. 6, 1990.

change along with most of the worlds leading nations.[43] This gave Gore another opportunity to show the rest of the nation and world the dangers of global warming and its effects upon our climate, and also afforded him more political capital and popularity. His star continued to rise, and his career was about to take off even higher.[44]

Al Gore worked closely with Senator John McCain (R-Arizona) in his days in the Senate, and in 1989 the two senators introduced legislation called the "Missile and Proliferation Act," which called for stopping he proliferation of ballistic missile technology, providing sanctions against nations that knowingly supplied advanced weapons and technology to other nations, such as Iran and Iraq, and also providing the President with authority to deny export licenses to defense contractors who violated the law. Gore stated that "Congress must act to make illegal traffic in these technologies very hazardous to the pocketbooks of certain kinds of corporations and their subsidiaries."[45]

While Senator Gore was a strong supporter of the military and weapons programs, it didn't prevent him from being aggressive with the Bush administration on foreign policy issues. During the Senate hearings on the buildup of the war with Iraq, Gore, along with his Democratic colleagues, questioned why the Bush administration and Defense Secretary Dick Cheney had not been forthcoming in its pronouncement that Iraq was close to having nuclear weapons. Gore said that the administration's pronouncements on Iraq's nuclear potential were "clearly misleading." The Bush administration had said that Iraq could potentially have a crude nuclear weapon within months. Gore challenged that assertion, saying that "Crying wolf is especially dangerous in the area of nuclear proliferation.", and had correctly concluded that Iraq's nuclear capacity was most likely many years down the road. It is ironic, looking back, that one of the administration's biggest proponents on Iraq's nuclear capability was Defense Secretary Dick Cheney, who would later, as Vice President under George W. Bush, make the same arguments for war with Iraq

43 Ibid.

44 Congressional Record, May 10, 1990.

45 Congressional Record, July, 1989.

in 2003.[46]It is also ironic that Al Gore was ahead of his time in his assessment of Iraq's nuclear capabilities, even years before the war.

On the night of January 11, 1991, Senator Al Gore was on the verge of making his biggest vote since he had been elected to the Senate in 1984. President George Bush had requested that Congress authorize force against Iraq and its dictator, Saddam Hussein, in response to Iraq's attack of Kuwait. Iraq had invaded Kuwait in a vicious attack that threatened stability in the Middle East and the world's oil supply. For Gore this was a very difficult decision to make. His own political party was pressuring him to vote against authorizing war with Iraq, urging him to, instead, support economic sanctions against Iraq, with the hope that diplomacy would prevent bloodshed. But deep down in his heart, Gore knew that liberating Kuwait and restoring peace would require using military force against Hussein and Iraq—not because of nuclear weapons, but because of Iraq's powerful military force. After hearing both sides of the debate, the Senator went home late that evening to sleep on it. The next morning, he made a speech on the floor of the US Senate saying that he would support authorizing military force against Iraq. He joined nine other Democratic Senators in voting 52-47 in supporting President Bush's resolution to declare war on the nation of Iraq. In his speech to the Senate on January 12, 1991, he stated that "The real costs of war are horrendous". "What are the costs and risk if the alternative policy does not work? I think they are larger, greater and more costly." Many of his friends and supporters point back to this vote as the finest hour in Gore's career. He had voted his conscience after careful deliberation despite intense pressure from both sides of the political isle, and he was at peace with his vote. Instead of hurting his chances for the presidency, his vote became an asset on his political resume.[47]

As a member of the Senate Armed Services Committee, Gore was very careful in how he voted. Before making a vote, he would go over testimony given in the Senate hearings, hold conference calls with civilian and military leaders at the Pentagon, review briefings

---

46 *Associated Press*, November 30, 1990.

47 *Time*, November 6, 2000, and Congressional Record, January 12, 1991.

from the president's national security team, and read the letters and transcripts of phone calls received from his constituents. Then he would spend hours going over all the data and information before making up his mind on a vote. His decision-making process was very deliberate, thoughtful, and pragmatic, much like the man himself. There were very few US Senators that had a better grasp of the political process than Al Gore; the only ones that came close to his ability were men that had served for over thirty years in the Senate. And no one worked harder or longer than Gore, not a single member in all of Congress. What he did for the people was remarkable indeed. And for that, the people of Tennessee were very proud, and they showed their great admiration for him when they re-elected him to the US Senate in 1990 by a 64 percent margin. Gore carried every single county in the state of Tennessee, something that had never been done before in the history of the state. This shows just how popular the moderate democrat was with the people of Tennessee, and his popularity continued to grow across the state and nation.

Over time, Gore's political philosophy would evolve to some extent. But it was difficult to place a label on Gore, as he was neither entirely conservative nor entirely liberal. He himself would later describe his political ideology as "raging moderate." In his early days in the United States House of Representatives, he was opposed to almost any form of gun control legislation, a position he campaigned on in 1976. But over time, and with societal changes demanding some attention, he would later change his mind and advocate for stricter gun laws. But even in the US Senate, he was considered a moderate on the gun issue and was not considered a threat to the National Rifle Association (NRA). Like many other southern Democrats, gun control was one issue in which he had to maintain a careful balance in how he voted. Gore's position on the abortion issue also evolved over time. When he was in Congress, he voted against federal funding for abortions, but he was always an advocate for women having the right to choose; he felt that abortions should be legal, safe, and rare. He was also a strong supporter of civil and equal rights, and believed that government should play a larger role in national issues, such as science, technology, and consumer and

environmental protection. He felt government involvement was necessary, in order to protect and enhance the lives of citizens. So while
Senator Gore was conservative on national defense and foreign policy issues, he was moderate to liberal on social issues and domestic
policies. In essence, Al Gore had become a national statesman, following in the footsteps of his father Senator Albert Gore, Secretary
of State Cordell Hull, Senator Estes Kefauver, and Senator Howard
H. Baker Jr., all Tennesseans who loved their state but also looked
out for the interests of the entire nation as a whole. Indeed, Al Gore
had become one of the best and brightest Senators in Washington,
developing a national following. His work and efforts had not gone
unnoticed, and it would only be a matter of time before he looked
at himself in the mirror to see if he saw the reflection of a future
President.

CHAPTER 6

First Presidential Campaign: 1988

The Democratic Party leaders could hardly hide their joy, as the end of the Reagan era was nearing an end, and after eight years of Republican rule, the Democrats were very anxious to take back the White House. Not only would the Republicans be without their great communicator, they would almost certainly be anointing Vice President George Bush as their nominee; the same George Bush who had gained a reputation as being a loyal vice president, but who had a personality that didn't inspire the masses, and who often times had a quick tongue. In other words, Bush was no Ronald Regan, and happier days seemed ahead for the Democrats. While most Democratic Party leaders were convinced of the party's prospects, the conservative wing of the Democratic Party was less than ecstatic. In fact, the party's moderate Democrats had formed a coalition called "the Democratic Leadership Council" (DLC), which was designed to enhance conservative legislation and elect conservative Democratic candidates in local, state, and federal elections. Another goal of the DLC was to nominate a moderate presidential candidate who could appeal to the independents and moderates of the electorate. Moreover, it was the DLC's belief that the Democratic Party had been nominating liberal candidates who ended up making too many promises to liberal special interest groups, resulting in the Republican Party becoming the American public's preferred party in presidential elections.

Regardless of the reasons, there was little doubt that Republicans had forged a winning formula in presidential elections. Since 1964, when President Lyndon Johnson was elected, the Democrats had won only one time thereafter, in the 1976 election of a southern governor named Jimmy Carter. Recognizing this, the DLC was convinced that in order to recapture the White House, the party must again turn to a southern candidate with moderate views. The DLC also developed and organized the "Super Tuesday" primaries in the south, which were conceived by the DLC as a way in which the southern Democrats could have a greater impact on the Democratic primaries. The hope was that the southern states would play a greater role in nominating a national candidate, while allowing a southern candidate to compete in the primaries. In the previous Democratic nominations, the Iowa and New Hampshire primaries had demanded more attention and created greater importance, simply because they were the first primaries in the nomination process, and thus their results played a greater role in determining the eventual nominee. There certainly wasn't a shortage of potential southern candidates in the Democratic Party. Senator Sam Nunn of Georgia; Senator Charles Robb of Virginia; Governor Bill Clinton of Arkansas; and Senator Dale Bumpers of Arkansas had all shown an interest in running for president. And they all had impressive resumes. Apparently many other Democratic Party leaders throughout the country were also convinced that a southern candidate would be what the doctor ordered. In late 1986, a prominent group of Democratic leaders formed a coalition in an effort to select a candidate to support during the Democratic nominating process. The name given to the group was "Impact 88," and the group's members had all pledged to raise $250,000 each for the candidate they endorsed. In March 1987, the group met to discuss the possibility of backing one candidate, but during the meeting the group fell into disagreement.

Then to everyone's surprise, seventeen of the members pledged their support behind Senator Al Gore of Tennessee. Nate Landow, a Maryland land developer and Impact 88 member, explained the rationale behind their decision: "He made the strongest impression of the candidates we interviewed. If Al Gore runs, he'll have strong backing."[48] If Gore had previously only been toying with the idea of running, the Impact 88 group caused him to seriously consider it. Maybe the time to run for President was at hand.

On March 24, 1987, the *Nashville Banner* ran a front-page story stating that Democratic fundraisers had approached Gore about becoming a presidential candidate. Gore dismissed the reports as only rumor. But the drama would continue. On March 27, the *Tennessean* ran a story about the possibility of Gore running for president. In the article, Gore was quoted as saying that he was "not a candidate" and was "not actively pursuing the possibility of running." But he quickly added that "the encouragement I have received increased substantially in the wake of Senator Bumpers's (of Arkansas) decision not to run. In the absence of any candidate from our part of the country, the nature of the encouragement is such that I feel that I am justified in giving some consideration to the possibility of becoming a candidate."[49]Clearly Al Gore was leaving the door wide open to a possible bid, and was now seriously considering the idea of running for president. Then, on the same weekend, Gore met privately with some of the members of Impact 88, and the meeting would prove to be crucial to Gore. Senator Gore was also a favorite candidate among the moderate Democrats in the south, including the DLC. Beyond that, the self-described "raging moderate" had built an impressive resume in Congress, with his populist views on domestic issues and his strong stance on national defense issues. Gores biggest problem in running for president in 1988 was his young age and his lack of name recognition. He was only thirty-nine, and had only been in the US Senate since 1984. But the positives far outweighed the negatives. Senator Gore had become known nationally, as a moderate Democrat who was a fighter for the people against big

48 Tennessean News Report, March 1987
49 Tennessean, 1987

corporations, who had authored important legislation on issues such as consumer protection, nuclear arms control, and the environment. Al Gore would be a strong candidate if he chose to run.

All eyes turned to the tiny little town of Carthage, neatly nestled in the Cumberland mountain region of north Central Tennessee, separated by hills and rivers. It is a typical border south town, populated with a hardware store and bank on one end of the corner square, and a drug store and clothing store at the other end. In the middle of the town square sits an old, redbrick, federal-style courthouse, with a white, ornate steeple that sits atop. It was built in 1877 and has had its share of big events. But on this particular hot summer day, in the summer of 1987, the people in the small town were gathered at the courthouse to witness something bigger than they had ever seen. There were busloads of men, women, and children being shuttled to the biggest event that Carthage had ever seen. As the people finally made there way to downtown, the entire courthouse square was now filled with thousands of loud and boisterous friends and supporters, all there for one single purpose. He was still inside the old, red-brick courthouse, looking over his notes while his family was waiting. Then he was ready, and he made a quick stride toward the front entrance of the courthouse, like he had done several times before, closely followed by his family. I remember seeing him in his navy blue suit and red tie as he came out of the courthouse, surrounded by his family. He smiled and waved to the crowd before finally heading to the podium, and then Al Gore finally said the words: "Today I'm announcing that I'm a candidate for President of the United States," as the crowd burst into applause, with many of the people crying in jubilation. It made one proud to be a Tennessean, to see one of its favorite sons running for the highest office in the land. The town of Carthage was very proud.

Gore quickly assembled a national campaign staff and began the long tedious process of conducting fundraisers across Tennessee and the south. By the summer of 1987, Senator Gore had forged together a viable campaign staff, and began to travel throughout the South, trying to shore up support and raise money. In a campaign swing through Texas, in August 1987, Senator Gore picked up several important endorsements from state-elected Democratic Party officials. He also attended a number of fund raisers in Dallas and other parts of the state. Former US Senator Ralph Yarborough, of Texas, was one of Gore's key supporters and introduced him at one of his campaign stops in the Lone Star State. Gore took to the podium and declared, "I'm here as a Tennessean, I'm here as someone from this area, the South and the Southwest." I believe very strongly that my candidacy offers the best chance of unifying our party. I believe I'm more electable than any of the other candidates." He also added, "I'm the raging moderate, a fresh start for America." This summed up Gore's main theme for the race.[50]

Senator Gore named Fred Martin as his campaign manager, and the Gore campaign began to formalize their national campaign strategy. This strategy called for Gore to bypass the Iowa caucuses, and focus instead on the Southern states and the Super Tuesday primaries. The Super Tuesday primaries would hold a total of twenty primaries on March 8, 1988, with more than 1,500 delegates at stake in the nomination process. Most of the states were in the southern region, where Senator Gore was clearly the early favorite candidate. Then, after a strong showing by Gore in the Super Tuesday states, he would try to ride the momentum to the nomination. Indeed being from the South was one of Al Gore's greatest strengths and his campaign's main strategy; he was a moderate democrat, from the South, who stood the best chance to win in the November elections. He and his campaign would remind the voters and Democratic Party officials that he was the best candidate at every opportunity they had. It was a plausible case, because the last two Democratic presidents to be elected (Johnson and Carter) were both from the South, and the last Democratic president who was not from the South was John F. Kennedy, in 1960, who won with the help of a southern (Lyndon Johnson) vice-presidential running mate, who was from Texas. So there was no question that for the Democrats to recapture the White House, Al Gore offered them the best opportunity in the November general election. But could a young, 39-year-old first-term Senator from Tennessee really win the nomination?

---

50 *Tennessean*, August 1987.

That was a question that could only be answered after the Super Tuesday election results.

As the campaign headed into the summer, the number of potential southern candidates began to dwindle. At the National Association of Counties convention, held in Indianapolis, Indiana, Arkansas Governor Bill Clinton made a speech. He was a very popular southern Democrat, and he received a roaring ovation from the audience, with many people saying they wanted him to run for president. But on Tuesday Governor Clinton announced that he would not be a candidate in 1988, and many of the convention attendees were openly disappointed that he would not be a candidate. Senator Gore spoke to the convention on Tuesday as well, receiving a very good response from the audience. Gore told the convention that "The New Federalism (Reagan Administration) has been nothing more than a raw deal for cities and counties throughout this land." And he pledged that as president, he would change that, and added that he would appoint a special assistant for county governments within his Cabinet. Gore also pledged to support welfare reform, and said he would not hold back federal money for highway and airport funds in order to make the federal deficit seem lower. After the speech his campaign held a reception, and there they signed up many volunteers.[51]

As the Gore presidential campaign proceeded, the first presidential debate was near. It was a hot day in Houston, Texas, where the Democrats were gathered for the nationally televised presidential debate. Senator Al Gore of Tennessee was anxious but prepared. He was ready to take to the stage and, for the first time, introduce himself to the entire Democratic Party and most of the nation at large. During the debate, Gore took center stage at times, passionately telling the audience that he was the best qualified and electable candidate in the democratic field. He stated that he was from the South and that if the Democratic Party wanted to win in November they should consider selecting a candidate who was a southern moderate like himself. Gore also expressed very pointed views on the role of the federal government, and what he thought was wrong with

---

51 *Tennessean*, 1987

the Republican administration. Gore seemed to catch his opponents off guard most of the night, and at times looked very commanding and presidential. After the debate he received very positive reviews. Larry Sabato, a political scientist from the University of Virginia, stated that "I have to say he was one of the most impressive. "I'd been programmed to believe he was too young." But Gore really projected. He looked more presidential than any of the others," Sabato said. Gore also scored points for taking on conservative moderator William F. Buckley over the cost of President Reagan's Star Wars program."[52]Gore had proved that he was indeed a formidable and viable candidate, and his debate performance would energize his campaign. It also sent a strong message to the rest of the Democratic candidates—Gore was serious about the race and would be a tough candidate in the primaries. On September 28, 1987, Gore campaigned in Georgia and picked up the support of Georgia Senator Sam Nunn, one of the most popular moderate democrats in the nation. While in Georgia, Gore made his case before a large crowd of voters. He stated that he was the only Democrat with a moderate record who could win the South and enable the Democratic Party to capture back the White House. He also made it clear that "no candidate could expect to win the Presidency without carrying the South."[53]

As the campaign kept pace, Gore continued to pick up key endorsements throughout the South from elected Democratic Party officials. In North Carolina he picked up the endorsement of former Governor Jim Hunt and former US Senator Terry Sanford. With the support of those two heavyweights, North Carolina looked secure. The momentum in the South would continue. In the state of Florida he picked up the endorsement of House Speaker Jon Mills, and in Texas he picked up the support of House Speaker Gib Lewis. A joint press conference was held in Washington to announce the endorsements from the two House Speakers from the two largest states in the South. "Both Mills and Lewis emphasized that they had considered all of the Democratic presidential hopefuls before deciding

---

52 *Tennessean*, 1987.

53 *Associated Press*, September 29, 1987.

on Gore. I have chosen Senator Gore because I feel he expresses the views of Texas, Texans and the rest of the nation,"[54] Lewis said. Mills stated that "this campaign provides vision and leadership for the "1980s" and beyond." At the press conference, Senator Gore was asked if he would settle for the No. 2 position on the ticket. He replied that "I would almost certainly turn it down". "Anybody who thinks I'm in this for anything other than the presidency is going to be surprised. We're in this race to win." If Gore could in fact win both Florida and Texas, he could make the argument that his campaign was not just regional; that would be the real test for Gore.[55]

By February 1988, the Gore campaign had spent a total of $891,320 in the Super Tuesday states, with a significant portion of that spent on television advertising. And it was estimated that the Gore campaign would spend as much as $3 million on the Super Tuesday states. The campaign was gambling all its hopes on Super Tuesday and the southern primary states.[56]The race for the Democratic nomination now turned to Iowa, but on this day Al Gore was nowhere to be seen in the state. The Gore campaign had early on made a calculated decision to forgo the Iowa caucus, believing that the winner of the caucus would not necessarily be the Democratic nominee. And the campaign strategy paid off. Congressman Richard Gephardt of Missouri won the Iowa caucus over a crowed field of Democratic candidates, winning with 31.3 percent of the vote to Senator Paul Simon's 26.7 percent. Both Gephardt and Simon were from neighboring states, and their regional appeal had given them the edge. Now the race would head into New Hampshire, where Governor Michael Dukakis (D-Mass) was the favorite-son candidate and expected to win.

The Gore campaign was also focusing on the New Hampshire primary, a state in which Gore had strong support. The campaign spent a total of $422,102 in New Hampshire in February, hoping that the senator could manage a strong second- or third-place finish, thereby giving his campaign some badly needed momentum heading

---

54 Tennessean, 1987

55 *Tennessean*, January 5, 1988.

56 Jim O'Hara, *Tennessean*, March 21, 1988.

into Super Tuesday. There were a total of twenty states holding primaries on Super Tuesday, and of those twenty, the majority were in the South and Southwest, and included: Arkansas, Alabama, Florida, Georgia, Kentucky, Louisiana, Mississippi, North Carolina, Oklahoma, South Carolina, Tennessee, Texas, and Virginia. There were more than 1,500 delegates at stake in the Super Tuesday primaries, and if one candidate could manage to win the majority of the delegates up for grabs, he would likely have the momentum needed to win the nomination. At the least, the southern primaries would narrow down the field of candidates. But what the Gore campaign and the DLC could not foresee was the sudden emergence of the Reverend Jesse Jackson. Jackson would prove to be Al Gore's primary competition in the South, and it was feared that he would win several of the Deep South states, thereby cutting into Gore's southern strategy. Such are the unknowns in politics. As the campaign headed toward Super Tuesday, Al Gore surprised everyone, winning the Wyoming caucus held on March 5. The surprise victory gave Gore much needed momentum heading into Super Tuesday.

It was now Tuesday, March 8, 1988. Super Tuesday had finally arrived. The stakes were very high, and the margin for error was very thin. For Senator Al Gore it meant that he needed to not only win the majority of the Southern States, but also overtake Governor Dukakis in the all important delegates. As the voters went to the polls on Super Tuesday, Gore and his campaign team were anxious. They knew from their private polling that the race would be very close in the southern primary states, with Gore battling Jesse Jackson for most of the states. The only question was voter turnout, and how many of Gore supporters would show up to vote. While a large turnout of Democratic voters would help Gore, it could also benefit Jesse Jackson in some areas of the South. Beyond that, there was a real possibility that Gore could win most of the states but would be forced to divide up the delegates, since the delegates were proportioned based on each congressional district. Finally, the primary votes began to come in just after 6:00 p.m. (EST), and Gore was glued to the television with his family and staff, watching the returns trickle in across the screen. The early results were looking very good for the senator, and he and his family and staff beamed with joy.

After the final votes came in, Gore managed to carry the border south states of Arkansas, Kentucky, North Carolina, Oklahoma, and his home state of Tennessee. He also, surprisingly, carried the Nevada caucus.

Meanwhile, the Rev. Jesse Jackson carried the Deep South states of Alabama, Georgia, Mississippi, South Carolina, and Louisiana. Governor Dukakis carried the key battleground states of Florida, Virginia, and Texas, along with Rhode Island and Hawaii. The Super Tuesday results were split. The delegate count now showed Governor Dukakis with 494 delegates, Jackson with 387, and Gore with 352. All of the other candidates had a combined total of 215 committed delegates. Since Governor Dukakis had carried the largest primary states and held a slight lead in delegates over Gore and Jackson, he was now perceived as the front-runner, and could lay claim that he was the only Democratic candidate who could win in all parts of the country. However, since there was a split of the delegates among three candidates, it made it unlikely that one of the candidates would be able to gain the majority of delegates to win the nomination. The race had been narrowed down to three candidates, and was now moving on to the Midwest. By winning several states and a large portion of delegates on Super Tuesday, Gore had surprised many who had doubted his strategy in the South. Gore now looked very clever, and his strong showing in the southern primaries gave him much-needed exposure and momentum. But, while the Gore campaign celebrated its victories, the reality was that Gore still had to win a majority of delegates outside the South, and that would prove to be much more difficult than his primary wins in the South. The Gore campaign was also facing a lack of funds, and found itself more than $1.7 million in debt; it desperately needed more money. With Governor Dukakis now the front-runner, it was becoming increasingly more difficult to raise money. The Gore campaign also looked at the electoral map and the national polling. It was very clear that he had not won enough southern states to become the front-runner, with Jesse Jackson being the main reason that he was unable to capture the majority of the southern states. Al Gore would now need to demonstrate that he could compete in the northern and midwestern states.

The race now moved on to Illinois, were Senator Gore traveled the day after the Super Tuesday primaries. As Gore arrived in Chicago, he told reporters, "I believe we can win a tremendous number of delegates here". "I think we are going to surprise people in Illinois when the returns come in here". "Gore's mood was one of gleeful vindication. As he settled into his chartered jet to fly into Chicago", the Senator said "Last night was all the sweeter because of the shovelfuls of dirt coming down on my head". "Some of them were kind of eating crow this morning." Gore also added this clear message at his democratic opponents: "Anybody who feels my message of standing up for working men and women is only going to play in the South, that conventional wisdom is wrong too."[57] There was much debate within the Gore campaign about whether he should compete in Illinois, with Campaign Manager Fred Martin arguing vigorously for Gore to skip Illinois and prepare for New York and California. However, it became clear that the state of Illinois was not likely to have much of an impact upon the outcome of the election. Senator Paul Simon was from Illinois and by all accounts would win the contest. So, privately the Gore campaign was hoping for a strong showing in the state, which would help them continue on in the race. On Election Day, Senator Simon won the state of Illinois, and the delegates were divided up among the three candidates according to how they fared in each congressional district.

The race for the Democratic nomination continued on, but unless things began to break for one of the candidates in the upcoming primaries, there was the real possibility that none of the candidates would win a majority of the delegates before the Democratic convention. This had the Democratic Party leaders worried, and many were concerned about the Reverend Jesse Jackson, because, while very popular in the African American community, he could also be a lightning rod nationally. There were a lot of headaches for the Democrats at this point in the race, and many party leaders wanted Senator Gore to get out of the race, in order to help Governor Dukakis's chances of winning. They shared the view that the longer that Gore remained in the race, the more likely Rev.

---

57 Jim O'Hara, *Tennessean*, April 16, 1988.

Jackson would stay in the race, thereby making it more difficult to keep him off the ticket once the Democratic Convention was held. But the Gore camp argued very strongly that it was too early to determine the likely outcome of the race, and until the results from the large states like New York and California were counted, it was premature to try to anoint one candidate.

Senator Gore's campaign staff believed that his next best chance to win was in the state of Wisconsin, with its primary on April 5. So they focused most of their attention and money on that key state, still holding out hope of an upset. While campaigning in Wisconsin, Gore compared himself to President John F. Kennedy, reminding the voters that it was Wisconsin that played a key role in electing President Kennedy in the Democratic primary of 1960. Gore told the voters of Wisconsin they had a chance to change the course of the campaign and elect him as President. In reminding the voters how Kennedy was able to win the race in 1960, Gore said, "All experts were proved wrong." "A big surprise took place in this state." Let's be honest. This race has evolved in a highly unusual way." "You can really elect me President."[58]

Al Gore lost in Wisconsin, finishing behind both Dukakis and Jackson. It was a huge disappointment, and it was now getting late in the game. Senator Gore now needed to make a Hail Mary pass or it would be the endgame. Thus the Gore campaign decided that their last stand would be New York and its 275 delegate votes. New York was also the second largest delegate state, and if Gore could pull off an upset there, he could still turn the race around. As the primary neared, Gore pulled off a major coup in New York, landing the endorsement of Mayor Edward Koch. The endorsement from Koch would prove to be both good and bad for Gore. While endorsing Senator Gore, Mayor Koch also blasted the Reverend Jesse Jackson as a "radical" that "only crazy Jews" would support. The Mayors comments were not received very well within the Democratic Party, or even by some of Gore's campaign staff and supporters. Mayor Koch introduced Al to a room of more than one hundred reporters. The Mayor also said he would campaign for Al throughout New

---

58 Bruce Dobie, *Nashville Banner*, April 1988.

York City. Indeed the city's large Jewish population had been prais-
ing Gore for several weeks and genuinely liked him and his stance
on Israel. But until Mayor Koch gave his public endorsement, many
had felt that he didn't have a legitimate shot in winning the nomination. Most Jewish voters also feared that a vote for Al Gore was a
vote taken away from Dukakis, and thus a benefit only to Jackson.
But Gore and Koch urged them to reject that reasoning and "vote
out of hope, not fear. Gore said, "It's not clever; it's the same kind of
thinking that's gotten this country in trouble in the past." New York,
with its forty-five electoral votes, would play a major role in helping
to shape the contest.[59]

The endorsement by Mayor Koch gave Gore's campaign
much-needed credibility and sent a strong message to the Jewish
community that Gore was someone they could trust. But it was
still a long shot at best for the young senator from Tennessee. On
April 19, the New York primary was held, and it would prove to
be bad news for Gore. Governor Dukakis won the state convincingly over Gore and Jackson, winning the majority of the delegates in the process. After New York, it was clear that Dukakis
was the man to beat, and for Senator Al Gore, the endgame was
now near.

While it was still possible that a brokered convention could
take place, the pressure was beginning to build on Gore to move
aside. If he did, then the odds were that Governor Dukakis could
win enough votes to go into the convention as the front-runner, and
with the delegates released from Gore, Gephardt, and Simon, he
would have a majority of the delegates needed to win. Finally, after
many days of deliberation and debate, the senator from Tennessee
decided that it was time to throw in the towel. He believed that if he
dropped out of the race then he would be a prohibitive favorite for
his party's nomination down the road, and that is exactly what the
Senator did. Al Gore bowed out graciously and vowed to support
the Democratic nominee. After the failed presidential bid, Gore was
forced to readjust to life in the US Senate. While most people would
settle for being a senator and be happy with that accomplishment,

---

59 Larry Daughtrey and Jim O'Hara, *Tennessean*, April 15, 1988.

Al Gore was not content, and he had unfinished business.[60] During the presidential bid, and with his surprisingly close finish, he had gotten a taste of what it was like in a presidential campaign, with all the national attention, and he liked it. It has been said that nothing compares to a presidential campaign, and the closer a candidate gets to the final prize, the more likely they crave to make it to the top. In Gore's case, he was in a great position, having finished a strong third and winning eight primaries. Al Gore had suddenly emerged as one of the Democratic Party's rising stars, and he would spend the next two years trying to tackle public issues that would further enhance his candidacy.

---

60 Nashville Banner

CHAPTER 7

Life in the Balance

On an April afternoon in 1989, Senator Al Gore and his son Albert III were preparing to leave Memorial Stadium in Baltimore, after attending an Orioles baseball game. In the blink of an eye, the six-year-old Albert suddenly pulled from his father's arm and darted out in the street in front of oncoming traffic. A car came rushing by and hit young Albert, throwing him thirty feet into the air. Senator Gore could only cry out with horror as he raced to his son's side. "By the time Al reached his son, the child was lying in a gutter, without breath or pulse having suffered massive internal injuries. The Senator just held his son and prayed" to God hoping that somehow his young son could survive the horrific accident. But it looked really bad, and as he went over to his son's side, his young son appeared lifeless.[61] "I don't know how many times I've relived those horrifying seconds, watching my precious child hurtle up and out of reach, as I squeezed my fist tightly in a futile effort to hold the little hand that

---

61 *Time*, July 20, 1992.

was already gone from mind," Gore would later say. "I have come to believe that we were literally in the company of angels that day."[62]

Thankfully, young Albert would make a full recovery after undergoing extensive treatment and hospitalization at Johns Hopkins University Hospital, in Baltimore. Al and Tipper would remain by Albert's side for several weeks, camped out at the hospital until he fully recovered. The experience was so emotional for the family, that Al and Tipper would undergo psychological counseling. "We grew tremendously by becoming aware of how we were dealing with it and how we were relating to one another in the midst of it." "I strongly recommend to any family undergoing an experience remotely similar to what we went through not to be afraid to do this," Gore would later say.[63]

While Albert III would slowly recover from his injuries, the incident would forever change the way that Al Gore looked at life and politics. It would cause Gore to reconsider his priorities in life. As he stated later: "Suddenly, the events that packed my schedule—once so seemingly urgent—were revealed as truly insignificant. I realized how trivial those events were that a month earlier had seemed so weighty and began looking at my whole life through the same new lens. I asked myself how I really wanted to spend my time on Earth. What really matters? "For me, the first answer was my family: my wife and my children. I made immediate changes to prioritize time with them—each one of them individually and all of us as a family together—in a way I had not done before."[64] This tragic experience had another effect upon Gore and his political career. While spending time at Johns Hopkins Hospital, with his son still recovering, Gore began writing a book on the environment and the consequences of global warming. He would spend the next two years writing, researching, and editing the book, with the help of Tipper, along with an entourage of scientists, professors, researchers, environmentalists, and personal friends. With his hectic Senate schedule and town hall meetings

---

62 Albert Gore, *An Inconvenient Truth* (2006), 68-69.

63 *Time*, July 20, 1992, pg. 29.

64 Gore, *An Inconvenient Truth*, 70.

back in Tennessee, it would become a big challenge, but in the end it was perhaps his greatest achievement and proudest moment outside of his family. The book, *Earth in the Balance*, would prove to be a best seller for Gore, both financially and politically. The book became the first book written by a sitting US Senator to make the *New York Times* best seller list since John F. Kennedy's *Profiles in Courage*. Gores fascination and sense of urgency with the environment caused him to make a bold political statement. This would bring him national attention and become a landmark book that would forever change Gore's image, but also the way people look at the environment. For Gore's critics, the book was an example of extremism. But among environmentalists and scientists, Gore would become a saint. Had Al Gore never accomplished another thing in his political career, writing this book would have been more than enough to leave a lasting legacy upon the world. His critics would later label him the "Ozone Man," and a tree-loving liberal. His book, however, would prove to be a political asset and, more importantly, become the landmark book that would forever cause the world to think about the environment in a global way, and to begin to look at the potential disaster that could happen if man failed to take action.

For many years in Congress, Senator Gore had demonstrated his interest in environmental issues. He had even written legislation to help protect the environment from the dangerous side effects of chemicals in our water and air, which ushered in a new era within the federal government. And he would use that expertise that he formed while investigating and conducting research into the environmental issues to form the basis for his book. The book allows one to analyze Gore's views not only on the environment, but also life.

Gore shared his personal thoughts about his desire to write the book after the near fatal accident of his son. "The life change has caused me to be increasingly impatient with the status quo, with conventional wisdom, with the lazy assumption that we can always muddle through. Such complacency has allowed many kinds of difficult problems to breed and grow, but now, facing a rapidly deteriorating global environment, it threatens absolute disaster. Now no one can afford to assume that the world will somehow solve its problems. We must all become partners in a bold effort to change the very foundation of our civilization."[65]

Al Gore grew up as a Baptist in the Bible Belt and was taught the fundamentals of being a God-fearing Christian. His parents also taught him to respect the earth and to be a good steward, and growing up on a farm only added to his respect and knowledge of how nature worked hand in hand with God and vice versa. Moreover, he learned the relationship between the land, the universe, and God. Al later attended Vanderbilt School of Theology, where he further developed a keen sense of spirituality and God's great creation: Earth. Gore said that writing the book was a personal experience that began more than twenty-five years before. While attending Harvard, he studied ecology and science, and it was one of his professors at Harvard that helped to inspire him to try to better understand the environment and the problems associated with it. In *Earth in the Balance*, Senator Gore shared with the readers why he was compelled to undertake the task of writing the book. He wrote: "I have been wresting with these matters for a long time. My earliest lessons on environmental protection were about the prevention of soil erosion on our family farm, and I still remember clearly how important it is to stop up the smallest gully 'before it gets started well'." "Our farm taught me a lot about how nature works, but lessons learned at the dinner table were equally important. I particularly remember my mother's troubled response to Rachel Carson's classic book about DDT and pesticide abuse, *Silent Spring*, first published in 1962. "But later during the Vietnam War, I encountered an even more powerful new poison, which was also welcomed at first". "I went to Vietnam with the army and vividly remember traveling through countryside that used to be jungle but now looked like the surface of the moon". "An herbicide called Agent Orange was the suspected cause of chromosomal damage and birth defects in the offspring of soldiers, I came to feel differently about it. Indeed, along with many others, I started to feel wary of all chemicals that have extraordinarily powerful effects on the world around us. How can we be sure that a chemical has only those powers we desire and

---

65 Albert Gore, *Earth in the Balance* (1992), 14.

not others we don't?"[66] Gore had made a very powerful statement about the dangers that threatened our environment.

In his opening introduction in the book, Gore summarized many of the things that all of us take for granted when it comes to the earth and nature. "The edifice of civilization has become astonishingly complex, but as it grows ever more elaborate, we feel increasingly distant from our roots in the earth. In one sense, civilization itself has been on a journey from its foundations in the world of nature to an ever more contrived, controlled, and manufactured world of our own imitative and sometimes arrogant design. And in my view, the price has been high. At some point during this journey we lost our feeling of connectedness to the rest of nature."[67]

Indeed the dumping of chemicals into the nation's rivers, streams, and oceans was one of the major problems that Gore outlined in his book. He argued that without major changes in the federal laws and educating the public, the world could face catastrophic consequences. While in Congress, Gore had been a leading advocate for environmental protection, and his book only reinforced his beliefs and sincere desire to help educate the public and government officials about the rising crisis. Al outlined in his book the key elements of what makes up what is now called "global warming" or climate change." He wrote that "the chemical and thermal dynamics of global warming are extremely complex, but scientists are looking especially carefully at the role played by one molecule: carbon dioxide (CO_2). Since the beginning of the industrial revolution, we have been producing increasing quantities of CO_2, and we are now dumping vast amounts of it into the global atmosphere." Beyond that, he explained "the correlation between CO_2 levels and temperature levels over time is well established. The greenhouse effect is, after all, a natural phenomenon that has been understood for more than a century. He then went on to state that the amount of carbon dioxide in the earth's atmosphere has risen over tens of thousands of years, and that by looking at the air bubbles that are trapped within

66 Gore, *Earth in the Balance*, 2.
67 Ibid.

the layers of ice, scientists can predict how the temperatures have changed over time".[68]

Gore stated that "it has been theorized by scientists that the recent warming trends throughout North America and much of the World are a result of two different phenomena; the first of which is the increasing deterioration of the earth's ozone layer, and the main source of this deterioration is thought to be fluoroclorcarbons, which are chemicals used in air conditioners and some plastic manufacturing processes. These chemicals are believed to be gradually suffocating the earth's ozone gases."

Moreover, Gore was also concerned with the increasing destruction of the world's rain forests, which were vital to the earth's plant photosynthesis. He was particularly concerned with the man-made destruction of the rain forest in Brazil, which accounted for approximately 40 percent of the world's rain forests. Gore said that with the destruction of the rain forests, carbon dioxide present in the atmosphere would increase and would contribute to the warming of the temperatures on earth.

Furthermore, Senator Gore explained that in Antarctica, the ice has melted dramatically the last forty years, another sign that the earth's temperatures had increased dramatically. And what was most disturbing about this fact was that Antarctica is one of the earth's keys to sustaining a balance between cold and heat. By the increasing melting of the ice, Gore said that it only adds to the climate crisis and speeds up the process. Indeed the book was alarming, and Al had effectively presented a case for governments taking immediate action to address climate change.

In *Earth in the Balance*, Gore also delves deeply into the spiritual aspect of nature and God; he makes a very strong argument that God and nature coexist, and he even believes that maybe we can see God's own image through his creation. "We are not used to seeing God in the world because we assume from the scientific and philosophical rules that govern us that the physical world is made up of inanimate matter in accordance with mathematical laws and bearing no relation to life, much less ourselves. Why does it feel faintly heretical to

---

68 Gore, *Earth in the Balance*.

a Christian to suppose that God is in us as human beings? Are we still unconsciously following the direction of Plato's finger, looking for the sacred everywhere except in the real world?" Gore further states: "It is my own belief that the image of God can be seen in every corner of creation, even in us, but only faintly. By gathering in the minds eye all of creation; one can perceive the image of the Creator vividly. "Similarly I believe that the image of the Creator, which sometimes seems so faint in the tiny corner of creation each of us beholds, is nonetheless present in its entirety—and present in us as well."[69]

Gore said that in order for our nation and the world to tackle the great environmental problems that we are facing now and in the future, we needed a plan, and he called for a "Global Marshall Plan" to help solve the problems. He outlined the many things that we can do to help solve the climate crisis and how the United States and all nations need to heed the warnings that are outlined in the book. With the writing of *Earth in the Balance*, Al Gore had accomplished a major milestone in his political career. One which would prove to be an asset as his career went forward, and one that would have a lasting legacy upon the world.

By the spring of 1991, Gore was wrestling with whether to make another presidential run against incumbent president George H. Bush, who was still popular with the voters after the successful War in Iraq, but who also was overseeing an economy at home that was starting to become a big concern. Gore, at only forty-three years old, was clearly one of the most popular candidates among the National Democrats and had become very popular with both liberals and conservatives within his party. He had become an authority on environmental issues, and continued to support consumer rights, labor groups, and unions. He also was one of the leading experts in the Senate on nuclear weapons and missile defense programs, having sponsored the US Nuclear Reduction Act, which called for a reduction in the number of nuclear warheads. And after his support of the War in Iraq, he had shown that he was strong on national defense and foreign policy issues. That would play well with the independent

---

69 Ibid.

swing voters in such crucial swing states as Ohio, Pennsylvania, and Florida. Add to that the fact that Gore would almost certainly be the favorite candidate in the southern states of Arkansas, Kentucky, North Carolina, and Tennessee, and any political spin doctor could make a great case for Gore running. Then there was the squeaky clean image of Gore, who was never involved in any political scandals and who had maintained a very public profile, along with his wife Tipper. Therefore, President Bush and the Republican Party would have a difficult time saying anything negative about Gore's military support and trying to paint him as a liberal Senator. Gore was the one man in Congress that President Bush did not want to face, and everyone inside the beltway knew it. There were also many prominent Democratic Party leaders urging Gore to run, among them Nate Landow, the Maryland Democratic Party Chairman who had supported Gore in his 1988 run. "He's an upperclassman in Democratic politics," Landow stated. "If he did get in, he would have a tremendously broad base of support." Jim Hall, a former aide to Gore's father, stated that "The times right for him. Al is just uniquely positioned. Like all politicians, he's ambitious. If you aren't ambitious, you aren't living much of a life."[70]

For Gore it was a time to reflect and determine if he still had the passion and drive to make another presidential bid. He said that the most important factor in making a decision would be his family and the time involved in running for president, but the time appeared to be right for him to make another run. The anticipation of his announcement was building, but to the surprise of Gore's friends and supporters, he announced later on in the year that he would not be a candidate for president in 1992. He cited his desire to spend more time with his family, and the accident that almost killed his son, as the main reasons for not making another bid at the time. Whatever the real reasons were, only Gore knows, but the fact remained he made a decision that appeared to cause his political career to veer off the road. But little did anyone know it was only a delay in Al Gore's political journey.

---

70 Judy Keen, *USA Today*, May 21, 1991.

CHAPTER 8

The Presidential Election: 1992

The race for the 1992 Democratic nomination was well under way in New Hampshire in February 1992, and Governor Bill Clinton of Arkansas was in a race for his life. After a series of scandalous stories (extramarital relationship, military draft issue, etc.) were leaked to the media, Clinton's poll numbers rapidly declined, and it appeared that his presidential hopes had faded. Senator Paul Tsongas of New Hampshire was the favorite-son candidate, and thus was expected to win the state. However, Bill Clinton needed to finish close behind, or his campaign was over. Thus Clinton took his campaign all across the state, making campaign stops in coffee shops, stores, factories, colleges, meeting and shaking as many hands as he possibly could. It was vintage Bill Clinton, the great campaigner with the energy and enthusiasm rarely seen in a politician. The more people he met the more momentum he received. As the election neared, Clinton's polls numbers began to improve, and going into the weekend before Election Day, it appeared that his hard work would pay off. On Election Day, Senator Tsongas won the New Hampshire primary, as expected, with Governor Bill Clinton finishing a strong second. Then the Clinton campaign went into political spin mode, and claimed that since Tsongas lived in Lowell, Massachusetts, he should have won. The national media concurred and did its own version of political spinning. It was just what Governor Clinton needed.

Now Bill Clinton was dubbed the comeback kid, and with the added media attention boosting his campaign, he was able to go into the southern primaries as the Democratic front-runner. He then won the Georgia primary on March 3, 1992, by a convincing margin, and was now the clear front-runner, with former California Governor Jerry Brown fading to a distant second. For Clinton the race had been long and hard, the fight difficult and exhausting. But finally it was time to put all the past behind him. With the Democratic nomination now assured, Governor Clinton began to look toward the general election. His next crucial test would be in his selection of a vice presidential running mate. The decision would be critical to him in his bid to win the White House, and his first real test since wrapping up the Democratic nomination. Clinton appointed Warren Christopher to head up his VP selection committee. Christopher was a high-profile attorney from Los Angeles who had been involved in Democratic politics for over four decades. He was a very bright but low-key man, with a deliberate approach to everything he did. Clinton had the perfect man for the job.

In April 1992, Senator Gore flew into Winchester, Tennessee, to speak to the Franklin County Chamber of Commerce, at the Regions Bank. Since I arrived at the bank before Senator Gore, I met one of my longtime friends, Mr. I. J. Grizzell, a prominent local banker and influential political supporter. Then I saw Chancellor Jeff Stewart, who comes from a famous political family. His father was a longtime chancellor, and his grandfather, Tom Stewart, was a United States senator in the 1940s and 1950s. Chancellor Stewart suddenly asked me if I wanted to accompany him to the Winchester Airport to pick up Senator Gore. I said sure, and we both headed out the side entrance where a police car was awaiting us. We drove out to the airport and waited on Senator Gore for about ten minutes. Then all of a sudden we heard the roar of the small Cessna plane as it approached the landing strip at the small airport. The plane slowly touched down and then taxied to the hangar where we were waiting. Then Senator Gore and two aides stepped out of the airplane and walked up to us. He greeted us warmly and we exchanged pleasantries. Then we hurriedly got into the police car and headed toward the bank. As we were driving along, I asked Al what he thought about Ross Perot's sudden rise in the presidential primaries. With a slight hesitation, he turned around and replied, "Well I think he is a very interesting character." I let out a chuckle and smiled, knowing that Senator Gore was being careful in his assessment of Perot and was, like the rest of us, not sure what to make of the little Texas maverick with the funny voice. Looking back I guess that I was not surprised by Senator Gore's careful worded comment. Neither Al nor any of us in the car had the slightest clue that in less than three months, Senator Gore would be right in the middle of the presidential campaign.

It was a typical hot summer July day in Carthage, Tennessee. For several days now, the people in the small town had been abuzz with rumor and speculation. The newspaper and television reports began swirling about its favorite son, Senator Al Gore, as a possible vice-presidential candidate. The reporters had camped outside of the Senator's home as the drama unfolded, but Gore would not give any hint about his name being mentioned. When he spoke to reporters, he smiled and said politely that he did not have anything to comment on. But the atmosphere of anticipation continued to fill the air in Tennessee and throughout the nation. The political drama finally came to an end the next day, on July 8, at around 11:15 p.m. Governor Bill Clinton telephoned Senator Gore, who was still at his home in Carthage with his family. Clinton politely spoke to the Senator, and then said "I want you to be my vice-presidential candidate." Al, without hesitation, stated that he would accept, and with that, Al Gore began a new journey.

"When Clinton made his decision on a Wednesday night at the end of a two-hour meeting, the Democratic nominee had been listening to the pro-and-con discussions on the merits of the six finalists (Gore, Indiana Congressman Lee Hamilton and Senators Harris Woodford of Pennsylvania, Bob Kerrey of Nebraska, Jay Rockefeller of West Virginal and Bob Graham of Florida). Suddenly, without fanfare, Clinton said, "I think I'm ready. I think I'm going to ask Senator Gore to run". "That low key moment brought to an end a search process that began with 40 names supplied by Warren Christopher and his team."[71]

In selecting Senator Al Gore of Tennessee, Clinton, from Arkansas, was going against the conventional political thinking that a running mate should be from a large state or a region different from the presidential candidate. Gore was from Tennessee, a neighboring state, and was also a white, moderate, baby boomer, just like Governor Clinton. However, those were some of the reasons that Clinton chose Gore. Al Gore was also very experienced in foreign affairs and nuclear weapons, and had a record in Congress that was very strong on the military and national defense. In addition, Al Gore had the squeaky clean image that Clinton didn't possess. Bill Clinton was also impressed with Gore's intelligence and grasp on the issues. He knew that Al was someone that could immediately step in and become president if something should ever happen to him. But in addition to Gore's resume, Clinton was also looking at the Electoral College map. He understood that in order to win the White House, he would need to carry several southern states. By selecting Senator Gore, Clinton calculated that he could win in Arkansas, Tennessee, Kentucky, and possibly Louisiana and North Carolina, states that Al Gore had performed extremely well in when he ran for president in 1988. The selection of Al also prevented the Republicans from trying to paint Clinton and Gore as liberals, since both were viewed as moderate democrats, which their public service records validated. This all added up to the decision that Governor Clinton ultimately made. Like Clinton, Gore also protested the Vietnam War, and anguished about the political consequences of resisting the draft. But Al had ultimately decided to join the Army in spite of his reservations. Gore would help Clinton with the environmentalists, for which he had become somewhat of a rock star after the release of his book *Earth in the Balance*. In his book *My Life*, President Clinton said of Senator Gore: "I believed his selection would work precisely because it didn't have the traditional kind of

71 *Time*.

balance. It would present America with a new generation of leadership and prove I was serious about taking the party and the country in a different direction. I also thought his selection would be good politics in Tennessee, the South, and other swing states. Moreover, Al would provide balance in a far more important way: He knew things I didn't."[72]

At the announcement in Little Rock, Arkansas, Gore stood side by side with Governor Clinton. After Clinton made his introduction, Gore took to the podium and stated, "I tell you truthfully, I didn't seek this....I didn't expect it. I'm here for one simple reason. I love my country."[73] A few hours later, slumped in a blue leather chair in the Governor's mansion, Clinton told *Time* some of the reasons that he chose Gore, and how he thought he would help him win. The selection of Gore proved to be very popular, as the public opinion polls showed. In a poll conducted days after the selection, 63 percent of the voters said that Gore was more qualified than Dan Qualye (earning 21 percent of the vote) to be president. There could not have been a clearer contrast than the experienced Gore against the gaffe-prone Dan Quayle, who was not ready for prime time.

It was just what the doctor had ordered for the Democrats. The 1992 presidential campaign was very important for the Democrats, with the party controlling the White House in only four of the last twenty-four years. Thus it was critical to the Democratic Party to turn the tide or else face the prospects of being the party out of power in the White House for another four long years. Bill Clinton was the southern governor of a traditionally conservative state, Arkansas, who had been viewed as a viable presidential candidate for several years, as he was a popular moderate Democratic governor in Republican territory. Clinton was also one of the best speakers and campaigners that the Democrats had seen in many, many years. He had a great ability to articulate his ideas very clearly, with great passion, and his charm was contagious and mesmerizing. He had the ability to personally connect with each voter, making them feel important, and it seemed his presence alone could cause people to

---

72 Bill Clinton, *My Life* (2004), 414.
73 Clinton-Gore Presidential Campaign Press Release, July 1992

like him. The Democrats had finally found their candidate, and the
excitement that Clinton generated had not been seen since John F.
Kennedy's campaign in 1960.

The Clinton–Gore campaign team was headed up by James
Carville, who was the campaign manager. George Stephanopoulos
and Paul Begala were the key political strategists, with Dee Dee
Myers the campaign's communications director. This group of political operatives and strategists were some of the brightest minds in
politics, and Governor Clinton would benefit greatly from their skill
and intellect. The campaign strategy early on was to paint President
George H. W. Bush as soft on the economy. The campaign slogan,
"It's the Economy Stupid," was derived from a phase made by James
Carville. The economy was now in a recession, with record numbers
of job losses and unemployment. President Bush didn't seem to have
a handle on the crisis, and it would prove to be his downfall. Clinton
and his team seized on this weakness and made it the central theme
of their campaign.

Al Gore proved to be an effective campaigner in the 1992 presidential election. Having gone through his own presidential bid in
1988, Gore was well suited for the intense schedule and media scrutiny that came with the race, and in many respects he was more
prepared for it than Bill Clinton himself. The Clinton–Gore team
took their message across the heartland of America. The campaign
decided that a bus tour across the Midwest—similar to the Truman
train tour in 1948—would send a clear message to the voters that
this was a generational election, with two young and bright candidates that would lead America safely into the twentieth century.

The bus tour proved to be widely popular and an effective strategy, as it allowed Clinton and Gore to meet the people up close
and face to face. They both took their wives, Hillary and Tipper,
with them on the bus tour throughout the heartland. Both couples
spent time talking about their families and politics, and genuinely
liked each other. Bill and Al both had many things in common, and
they really bonded on the bus tour, spending hours talking about
politics and their vision for the country. They campaigned almost
nonstop, stopping only at night to sleep for a few hours. Across the
Midwest, they were met by Democrats, Independents, and even

some Republicans that were craving for change. The economy was as bad as ever, in the worst recession since the Great Depression. Thousands of people turned out at each of the campaign stops. They met with soccer moms, suburbanites, young college students, the elderly, farmers, and small businessmen. At one stop on the tour, "Al Gore asked voters to think about what headline they wanted to read the day after the election: 'Four More Years,' or 'Change' is on the Way." The audience focused on the right answer, and change was on the way. The bus tour would continue up until the Democratic convention in New York City, and each passing day the tour became a bigger event, with throngs of people turning out to meet Clinton and Gore and various stops.

Now it was time to turn to the 1992 Democratic Convention, where Governor Clinton and Senator Gore would have their biggest challenge yet. It was a time to demonstrate to the country they were the candidates of change and hope. The stakes were very high, and the eyes of the nation were focused upon them. The Democratic convention was held at Madison Square Garden, in New York City, July 13-16, 1992. As the convention neared, the pressure started to build for both Clinton and Gore. For Bill Clinton, the convention and acceptance speech would be his opportunity to show the nation his vision for change. And for Al Gore, it would be a test to show if he could live up to the expectations that had been placed upon him since becoming Clinton's vice-presidential running mate. The jingle and jangle of noise was everywhere in the convention hall. The Democratic delegates were bursting with joy as they awaited the nomination of Governor Bill Clinton and Senator Al Gore for president and vice president.

Al Gore made his acceptance speech on Wednesday, July 15, 1992. He made a very passionate and emotional speech about his family, life, and career, and ended his speech by telling the audience about his son Albert III's tragic accident. Al spoke in a quiet, deliberate tone as he described the horrifying events on that terrible day in Baltimore. He said that the near death of his son had changed his outlook on life forever. By the end of the speech, he had most of the convention in tears. The audience then burst into loud applause. Gore had given the speech of his life, and he demonstrated that Clinton had made a wise choice in selecting him as his running mate. The pace had now been set.[74]

Now it was time for Bill Clinton to make his case before the American people. And the man from Hope, Arkansas, didn't disappoint. In fact, he delivered a speech that was considered one of the best in the history of political nominations. He talked about growing up poor in a broken family in rural Hope, Arkansas, and of the people that had made an impact upon his life. And he described how he was able to rise above his family's poverty, through education and hard work. His speech was framed in a way that showed how deeply he cared about the poor and working class people of society. And he showed that if a poor boy from Hope, Arkansas, could be nominated for president, it showed that the American dream could still be achieved. It was one of the most profound political speeches in history. Bill Clinton had made the speech of his life, had mesmerized the Democratic convention, and had impressed the American public. His convention speech would propel his candidacy and provide a significant poll bounce. Bill Clinton was now the front-runner.

President George Bush and the Republicans were worried, and they went into a full-frontal assault to try to turn the race around. President Bush had seen his popularity plummet since the Persian Gulf War, due to the growing public perception of an economic recession. The president's popularity began falling throughout late 1991. By January 1992, his approval ratings fell below 50 percent and would continue to fall. By the time of the election campaign, his ratings were at an all-time low. The president now needed to turn the race around, and he would try to use the upcoming presidential debates to begin his comeback. The campaign now turned to the debates, and Senator Al Gore was more than ready. The first vice-presidential debate took place on October 13, 1992, in Atlanta, Georgia. Gore would face off against Vice President Dan Qualye and Admiral Stockdale, Ross Perot's running mate. The moderator was Hal Bruno of ABC News. Mr. Bruno introduced the vice-presidential candidates and described the debate's format in his opening remarks. Soon after the debate began, Al Gore blasted off with

---

74 CNN News, July 15, 1992

strong remarks about the Bush administration. He was not shy in telling the American people that the last four years under President Bush were really bad.

Gore stated that "Bill Clinton's top priority is putting America back to work". "Governor Clinton and I will create good, high-wage jobs for our people, the same way he has done in his state". "He (Clinton) has created high-wage manufacturing jobs at 10 times the national average and in fact according to the statistics coming from the Bush–Quayle Labor Dept, for the last 2 years in a row (Arkansas) has been number one among all 50 in the creation of jobs in the private sector. "By contrast, in the nation as a whole, during the last 4 years, it is the first time since the presidency of Herbert Hoover, which we have gone for a 4-year period with fewer jobs at the end of that period than we had at the beginning". Gore had made a very pointed example of the nation's economic decline under the Bush administration. He also said "We have lost 1.4 million jobs in manufacturing under George Bush and Dan Quayle".[75]

In one of the more pointed exchanges between Gore and Qualye, the senator slammed the vice president on the abortion issue. When Qualye stated that Gore and Clinton were for abortion, Al pounced back. "Well, you notice in his response, that Dan did not say I support the right of a woman to choose. That is because he and George Bush have turned over their party to Pat Buchanan and Phyllis Schlafly, who have ordered them to endorse a platform which makes all abortions illegal under any circumstances, regardless of what has led to that decision by a woman. Even in cases of rape and incest, their platform requires that a woman be penalized, that she not be allowed to make a choice, if she believes, in consultation with her family, her doctor, and others, whoever she chooses, that she wants to have an abortion after rape, or incest. They make it completely—Vice President Quayle then retorted: Senator do you support a 24-hour waiting period? Senator Gore then said "illegal under any of those circumstances."[76] The debate waged on and Al

---

75 CNN News Broadcast, July
76 Ibid.

Gore continued to discredit the vice president and the Bush administration, while both candidates basically ignored Admiral Stockdale.

By all accounts, Gore won the debate. It wasn't even a close
contest. He was able to demonstrate how President Bush and Vice
President Qualye were extremists who were too conservative for the
majority of Americans, and out of touch on the issues. Al Gore had
showed his policy expertise and debating skills. Governor Clinton
was smiling, and President Bush was blushing. After the Democratic
convention, both the Clinton and Bush campaigns waged a war of
words in television ads across the nation. Suddenly, then, both campaigns were stunned with the news that Ross Perot had decided to
quit the race.

The surprise announcement shocked Perot's supporters, yet
energized the Clinton and Bush camps. Both campaigns tried to
seize the moment and pick up as many of the Perot supporters as
they could. One can only assume the reasons why Perot opted out
of the race. But his exit created much buzz, with Bill Clinton and
Al Gore convinced that they would benefit more. As the campaign
went into full swing throughout the fall, the Bush campaign began to
personally attack Bill Clinton on his character and credibility. They
used the Gennifer Flowers and Paula Jones scandals to illustrate that
Clinton's character was bad. In addition, they said he had been a
draft dodger during the Vietnam War. But Governor Clinton's campaign would fire back every time at President Bush, accusing him
of trying to change the debate in order to hide his failures as resident. Meanwhile, the Clinton campaign focused their attention on
the economy, and President Bush's lack of leadership, which was of
far more political relevance. They went full force at the president
and never looked back. The campaign continued, with Bill Clinton
maintaining a slight lead through September.

Then to everyone's surprise, Ross Perot decided to re-enter the
campaign, and the race began to tighten once again. Initially the
Bush campaign welcomed the news, theorizing that Perot would
most likely take potential votes away from Clinton. However, as the
weeks passed by, it became clear that President Bush wasn't moving up much in the polls, and so Governor Clinton continued to
maintain a slight lead over President Bush and Ross Perot as the

campaign neared the homestretch. The Clinton campaign continued to focus on the economy, emphasizing how President Bush had failed in his domestic policies. As the campaign neared its conclusion, the public opinion polls indicated that the Clinton strategy was working. With Bill Clinton now leading in the polls by four to five percentage points, it was a matter of finishing the race without making any major mistakes. Indeed it was Clinton's election to lose. Going into the final weekend of the campaign, the Bush camp could only hope and pray. The national polls showed Governor Clinton with an almost insurmountable lead, anywhere from five to seven percentage points. Bill Clinton and Senator Gore were confident that they would win the race. All of the campaign's private polls showed a solid lead. It was their race to lose, and only a miracle could keep President Bush in office.

Then finally they were ready. Election Day had arrived, and the Clinton–Gore campaign gathered in Little Rock, Arkansas. All across the land, from the cornfields of Iowa, to the busy streets of Los Angeles, millions of Americans went to the polls, exercising their power and will over the most important election in the world. It was a day in which the ordinary citizen had as much power as the elite in society, in which power was exercised in non-violent ways. What began with a few votes in a small village in New Hampshire, just after midnight, quickly turned into a mass of millions cast across the vast parts of the United States. By the time the polls closed on the West Coast, just after 9:00 p.m. (EST), almost ninety-five million people had cast a vote for the presidency.

As the election results began to trickle in, Clinton was performing extremely well in New England and the border south states. Shortly after 7:00 p.m. (EST), Governor Bill Clinton was declared the winner in most of the New England states. He was also declared the winner in several key states, such as Tennessee, Kentucky, and West Virginia. As the election night proceeded, Clinton and Gore were performing extremely well with the voters in the rural areas of the South and Midwest, winning in Arkansas, Missouri, Louisiana, Georgia, Iowa, North Carolina, and Virginia. Many of these states were traditionally Republican strongholds and would prove to be the key to victory. Slowly, as the hours went by, the electoral votes began to accumulate for Bill Clinton. Now all eyes turned to the key bell-wether states of Ohio and Florida. Both states were vitally impor-tant to both Governor Clinton and President Bush, not only from an electoral advantage, but also from a historical standpoint. The significance was very great, since no Republican candidate in recent history had won the presidency without carrying Ohio. By the time the Ohio polls closed, all the television networks announced that Bill Clinton would win the state by about 90,000 votes, less than 2 percent of the vote. Clinton was also declared the winner in Florida, and now winning both the battleground states of Ohio and Florida, it became clear that Clinton was almost certain of victory. By 9:00 p.m. (EST), the national television networks had called the race for Governor Bill Clinton of Arkansas. The American people had spo-ken loud and clear.

Bill Clinton and Al Gore had won convincingly, beating President Bush by 43 percent to 37 percent, with Ross Perot receiving 19 per-cent of the vote; the Clinton–Gore ticket won thirty-two states, with the remaining eighteen states going to President Bush. And in the Electoral College, they had won in a landslide, winning over 370 of 538 electoral votes. Bill Clinton was the next President of the United States. The American people had turned out in record numbers, with over one hundred million votes cast, the highest percentage of votes cast since the 1960s. Clearly the American people wanted change, and the vast majority believed the right choice was Clinton and Gore. The possibility of happier days for the Democrats and the nation was almost more than they could imagine. It was a time for celebration, and for Al Gore, it was another step up the political ladder.

It was a cold, but sunny day in Washington, DC on this January winter day. Al Gore and Bill Clinton were both anxious, and in a few more hours they would have more responsibility and attention than they probably ever dreamed of. But on this day, it was time to celebrate and enjoy the moment, before their lives would be forever changed. January 20, 1993, was the day in which William Jefferson Clinton and Albert Gore Jr. took their respective oaths of office, as President and Vice President of the United States. Their fam-ily, friends, and supporters had all gathered in the nation's capital to witness the event. It was a day that the United States of America peacefully transferred the powers of the offices in an orderly and dignified way. I will never forget that cold day in Washington, watching Clinton and Gore being sworn in office. Throughout our nations history, it seems that the right leaders always emerge at the precise time when the country needs them the most. And looking back now I see a nation that was on the cusp of change, and the perfect leaders for that change where President Bill Clinton and Vice President Al Gore.

1976 Al Gore Jr. Campaign for Congress

YOU ARE CORDIALLY INVITED TO ATTEND
A RECEPTION FOLLOWING THE

CONSTITUTIONAL OATH

OF

ALBERT GORE, JR.

UNITED STATES HOUSE OF REPRESENTATIVES
FOURTH DISTRICT OF TENNESSEE
ON TUESDAY, JANUARY 4TH, 1977
2 P.M. TO 5 P.M.
B-354 RAYBURN HOUSE OFFICE BUILDING
WASHINGTON, D.C.

R.S.V.P.   RT #2, CARTHAGE, TN

**Congressman Al Gore Jr. and Author Troy Gipson. Franklin
County High School Graduation, 1980. Winchester, TN.**

**Congressman Al Gore and Author, Winchester,
Tennessee December 1983**

1984 US Senate Campaign Brochure

**Senator Al Gore Presidential Campaign Super Tuesday
Victory Speech, Nashville, Tennessee 1988**

The Presidential Inaugural Committee
requests the honor of your presence
to attend and participate
in the
Inauguration of
William Jefferson Clinton
as
President of the United States of America
and
Albert Gore, Jr.
as
Vice President of the United States of America
on Wednesday, the twentieth of January
one thousand nine hundred and ninety-three
in the City of Washington

Vice President and Tipper Gore, Nashville, Tennessee 1994

Happy Birthday Al, Nashville, Tennessee 1994

**Vice President Gore and President Bill Clinton, 1996
Democratic National Convention Chicago**

Vice President Al Gore

Official Photo

Gore 2000 Campaign Memorabilia

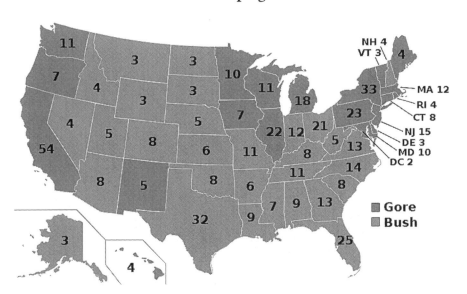

Vice President Gore and author, Nashville, Tennessee
Vice President Al Gore, Nashville TN Dec. 1996

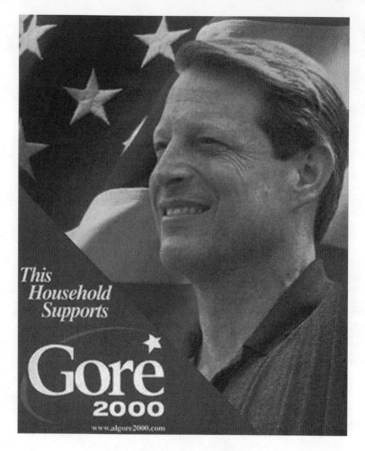

Gore 2000 Campaign Poster

For my great
friend, Troy Gipson,
with best wishes and
many thanks,

Al Gore

Al Gore speaking on Climate Crisis

Al Gore Nobel Peace Prize Speech

CHAPTER 9

The Vice Presidency: 1993–1997

It was now day one for President Bill Clinton and Vice President Al Gore. While the 1992 Presidential Campaign had been a roller coaster of a ride, both men now faced the reality of being the most important leaders of the nation and much of the world. Most men never dream of a life of power at this level, and the ones that do rarely ever face it. There is nothing that can really prepare one for the awesome power and responsibility of being President and Vice President of the United States. It was indeed an awesome responsibility and undertaking, but Clinton and Gore were both well prepared and suited for the long ride into history.

During his years as vice president, Gore was an extremely active participant in the Clinton presidency. Clinton would delegate more responsibility to Gore than any other president has delegated to a vice president in history. He held a weekly one-on-one lunch with him, and also placed Gore inside his inner circle of advisors. There were very few major decisions made by President Clinton that did not include some input from Vice President Gore. This was a wise decision and made the vice president relevant in the administration. Gore seized the opportunity and worked extremely hard in his job. He didn't always agree with the president, and was never afraid to disagree with him. But he was also very loyal and always supported the President publicly in his decisions. President Clinton trusted him, and encouraged Gore to be totally frank and honest with him during his entire Presidency. Gore's role grew out of the working relationship and genuine friendship that he developed with presidential-candidate Clinton during the 1992 campaign. The two men genuinely liked each other, and that carried over into the presidency. President Clinton also trusted Gore's advice and counsel when it came to dealing with Congress. He knew that the vice president had a lot of experience with Congress, and he valued the many accomplishments Gore achieved while in the House and Senate. He also saw the vice president as his future successor. At his very first cabinet meeting, Clinton made it clear that when Vice President Gore spoke, he was also speaking for the president. It was a clear message to the entire cabinet, and it did not go unnoticed. In his book *My Life*, President Clinton talks about how vital Al Gore was to his presidency: "Al Gore helped me a lot in the early days, encouraging me to keep making hard decisions and put them behind me, and giving me a continuing crash course in how Washington works. Part of our regular routine was having lunch alone in my private dining room once a week." "We took turns saying grace, and then proceeded to talk about everything from our families to sports, books, and movies to the latest items on his agenda or mine." "Though we had a lot in common, we were very different, and the lunches kept us closer than we otherwise would have been in the Washington pressure cooker, and eased my adjustment to my new life."[77]

Shortly after taking over as vice president, Gore was tapped by Clinton to head up a presidential review of the federal government, called the "National Performance Review" (NPR). The review was unique and was designed to perform a comprehensive review across all government agencies and spending areas within the US budget and governmental networking. Gore was given

---

77   Bill Clinton, My Life (2004), 516.

sole responsibility for leading the review and reporting back his findings and recommendations to President Clinton. This was the first legitimate attempt by any president to look at the complex federal government and try to find ways in which to save time and money. President Clinton made a very high-profile announcement to the public about the review, with Gore at his side. Vice President Gore and his team began the process of conducting the review on March 3, 1993.

The team spent the next six months gathering information from across all facets of the US government, including agencies at the federal, state, and local levels; federal employees; government contractors; and private citizens. They also received and read more than thirty thousand letters and phone calls from citizens across the country. In addition, Gore's committee brought together leading experts from government, industry, academia, and the private sector to obtain their ideas and input into how to improve the federal government, with the emphasis on saving time and money and enhancing efficiencies. The vice president and his team then made a long list of recommendations on how to proceed with implementing the changes that were outlined in the report. Vice President Gore and his team did a fantastic job. At the end of the review, Gore stated that "the report represents the beginning of what will be—what must be—an ongoing commitment to change. It includes actions that will be taken now, by directive of the President; actions that will be taken by the cabinet secretaries and agency heads; and recommendations for congressional action. The National Performance Review focused primarily on *how* government should work, not on *what* it should do. Our job was to improve performance in areas where policymakers had already decided government should play a role." [78]

The review called for reducing waste, eliminating unnecessary bureaucracy, improving services to taxpayers, and creating a leaner, more productive government. The review also recommended the use of information technology and other techniques to increase opportunities for early, frequent, and interactive public participation during

---

78   Albert Gore, "Creating A Government that Works Better and Costs Less: Report of the National Performance Review," September 7, 1993

the rulemaking process and to increase program evaluation efforts. It also called for streamlining management control; improving customer services; improving financial management; and overhauling the federal procurement and support services. In all the report estimated that some 100 billion dollars in federal expenses could be cut or eliminated. Vice President Gore formally submitted the report to President Clinton at a public announcement on September 7, 1993, which was attended by the media and various citizens and employees who had taken part in the intensive review. The next day, on Sept. 8, 1993, Gore accompanied President Clinton to a White House press conference and photo shoot. There Vice President Gore formally announced some of his findings and recommendations, and stated that the government review could result in savings of $108 billion over five years. The plan specifically called for "reduction of the federal workforce by 252,000 over 5 years; closing and consolidating 1,200 Agriculture Field Offices and reducing 7,500 employees, and enact federal budgets every 2 years instead of every year, among other proposals. "The Government is broken," President Clinton said, and "we intend to fix it." Gore called government "old fashioned, outdated. [It's] using a quill pen in the age of WordPerfect." Overall the plan called for eliminating 12 percent of the non-postal federal jobs over five years.[79]

Early in 1993, the Clinton administration proposed a trade initiative with Canada and Mexico. It was called the North American Free Trade Agreement (NAFTA). The initiative was designed to eliminate trade barriers between the three North American countries. There were many critics of this proposal, among them unions and small businesses, which were traditional Democratic constituencies. In fact there seemed to be more support for NAFTA from the moderates and conservatives than any of the voters. Thus the NAFTA issue was not a popular move with the liberals of the Democratic Party. Congress was divided on this issue, with most of the support coming from moderate democrats and conservative republicans. President Clinton knew it would be a difficult sell to Congress and the public, so he decided that he would turn to Al Gore to be the spokesman for the administration on this issue.

---

79   Ibid.

Gore took the debate to the American people on a live televised debate with former presidential candidate and nemesis Ross Perot. The vice president debated Perot on *Larry King Live* on November 11, 1993. Vice President Gore arrived in the CNN studios about a half hour before the debate. He was well prepared and confident, but unusually nervous. Wendy Walker, the producer of the show later recalled, "Al looked extremely anxious". "He seemed to be on edge about his debate".[80] However just minutes before he went on the air, his aide Bob Squier whispered something to the Vice President, which caused him to loosen up and laugh. The pep talk sure didn't hurt, and maybe even helped.[81] Al Gore could not have been better in his debate with Perot, effectively making the the case for support of NAFTA. He explained that it would bring millions of new jobs to the US economy, while also improving the nation's relationship with Canada and Mexico. He argued its merits very effectively, and immediately caught Perot off guard by taking the debate to him and putting him on the defensive. In doing so, Gore once again showed off his great skills in debating. By almost all accounts, Gore overwhelming won the debate over Perot, and in so doing turned the tide in favor of the Clinton administration. The vice president's performance was widely accepted as the turning point in the NAFTA issue. The public opinion polls went from around 35 percent to over 65 percent in support of NAFTA after the Gore-Perot debate.

It was Al Gore that had paved the way for passage of NAFTA. The Clinton administration then proceeded to have the Democratic Congress formally introduce the NAFTA bill for vote. The House of Representatives voted on the bill on November 17, 1993, with the bill passing 234–200. The US Senate passed the bill by an even wider margin, 61–38. President Clinton signed it into law on December 8, 1993. Without Gore's superb debate performance, it is likely that the bill would not have been passed by Congress. Years later, Larry King pointed out that the Gore–Perot debate was one the more memorable events in his life.

---

80   "Producer", by Wendy Walker, 2010.

81   Ibid

The other most significant accomplishment in Gore's first year as vice president was his deciding vote on the 1993 Federal Budget Amendment, better known as the Omnibus Budget Reconciliation Act of 1993. Since the United States Senate was deadlocked on the matter, with the vote tied 50–50, it was Vice President Gore, as the residing Officer of the US Senate, who broke the tie, which ended up giving President Clinton and the administration its first major legislative achievement. The Senate passed the act on the last day before their month-long vacation, on Friday, August 6, 1993, by a vote of 51–50 (fifty Democrats plus Vice President Gore voting in favor). The passage of the 1993 federal budget was historic in that it created a positive impact upon the economy for the next several years. It also included tax relief for fifteen million working families through the expansion of the earned income tax credit, and helped millions of children who were living with families in poverty. Another significant piece of legislation had been made by President Clinton, and Vice President Gore had played another key role in the success. In May 1994, President Clinton asked Gore to fill in for him on a trip to South Africa for Nelson Mandela's Presidential inauguration. Hillary Clinton and Tipper also accompanied the Vice President on the trip. It was a moving experience to be part of history in the making, as they watched Mandela take over the Presidency after so long a personal struggle in his fight for freedom in South Africa.[82]

Near the end of the first year of the Clinton Presidency, President Clinton and Vice President Gore confronted a controversial, yet important piece of legislation dealing with gun control. The gun control issue had been a concern for many years, but it became a national debate after the attempted assassination of President Reagan in 1981. James Brady, Reagan's press secretary who was wounded and left paralyzed after the shooting, began a national campaign to restrict the purchases of hand guns. Then after many years of public debate, Congress finally picked up the proposal through the introduction of the "Hand Gun Violence Prevention Act", later known as the Brady Bill. The proposed law required, among other things, background checks of individuals before a firearm could be purchased

---

82   Hillary Rodham Clinton, *Living History*, 2003

from a dealer, manufacturer or importer. President Clinton and Vice President Gore both supported the Brady Bill, and after Congress passed the legislation, President Clinton signed the bill into law on November 30, 1993, with it going into effect in January 1994. Then later on in 1994, the Congress introduced another gun control proposal in a bill called the "Federal Assault Weapon Act", which the President Clinton and his Administration strongly supported. The law called for the ban of manufacture and purchase of certain types of semi-automatic firearms, including assault rifles and machine guns. The law was passed by both the U.S. House and Senate and signed into law by President Clinton on September 13, 1994. The decision by President Clinton and Vice President Gore to support both of the gun control laws would prove to be very unpopular within certain elements of the public, but especially the National Rifle Association (NRA) and the National Republican Party. They would use the gun issue in their campaign against the Democrats in the 1994 Congressional elections, and also in the future Presidential elections. And it would also be an issue that would cause Al Gore to pay a high political price for his support.[83]

Vice President Gore was also instrumental in foreign policy in the Clinton administration. President Clinton appointed Gore to head up the US-Russian nuclear arms talks. In this role, Gore effectively demonstrated his foreign policy expertise. He was particularly effective in enhancing relations with the United States and Russia. The vice president made several trips to Russia during his first term as vice president and had a memorable meeting with Russian President Vladimir Putin during one visit.

Gore was also active in a number of environmental initiatives in Clinton's first term. He initiated the GLOBE program on Earth Day in 1994, which used education and science to increase public awareness of the environment. Gore would continue to focus much of his attention on environmental and consumer issues throughout the rest of his first term.

While Gore was given much responsibility from President Clinton, he made it a point to never upstage Clinton. Gore demanded

---

83   US Congressional Record, September 1994

loyalty from his own staff, and so he made sure that he and his staff were always publicly in sync with the president and his staff. There were times where the vice president disagreed with President Clinton, but he always went about it in a constructive way, knowing that President Clinton valued his opinion more than anyone else within the cabinet. Gore would sometimes outline other options on issues that were sometimes debated by the president's cabinet.

In 1996, President Clinton signed into law the Telecommunications Act, which was a sweeping overhaul to the industry, and something that Vice President Gore had crafted and pushed for. The act also "increased competition, innovation, and access to what Al Gore called the 'information superhighway'…It also contained a requirement that new television sets include the V-chip, which… [allowed] parents to control their children's access to programs."[84] Vice President Gore was instrumental in the Telecommunications Act and had persuaded President Clinton to include language about the V-chip, along with Internet-related language.

It was now 1996, and the Clinton re-election campaign was in full swing. The Republican Party front-runner was Senator Bob Dole of Kansas, a longtime US senator who was a World War II veteran and well-respected politician, and senior party statesman. Senator Dole went on to capture the Republican nomination with little opposition. But the biggest problem facing Senator Dole would be the economic prosperity that the nation was experiencing under President Clinton and Vice President Gore. In addition to Senator Dole, Ross Perot also became a candidate, running as an independent. Perot used the same arguments that he had made in the 1992 campaign, but this time the American people were not as excited about his candidacy. During the summer months, both campaigns began running campaign ads and campaigning across the nation. Senator Dole's campaign began to run negative attacks on President Clinton, calling into question some of the personal scandals like Whitewater that had plagued the President almost immediately after he took office. Senator Dole went out of his way to tell the American people that they needed a President they could trust. But this argument

---

84 Clinton, *My Life*, 699.

was not very effective, and as the campaign approached the National Convention, Senator Dole found himself in an uphill battle. Prior to the Republican National Convention, Senator Dole selected Jack Kemp, the former Congressman and ex-NFL Football great, as his Vice Presidential running mate. The selection of Kemp was received very well by the media and American people as a solid choice, and Senator Dole had delivered in his first real test of the campaign.

The election headed into the 1996 national political convention, with President Clinton enjoying a comfortable lead of twelve to fourteen points in most national polls. At the 1996 Democratic National Convention held in Chicago, Gore took to the podium and made a very passionate speech. He talked about the success of the past four years under the Clinton administration, and outlined the things he and President Clinton planned to do in the next four years. He also spoke about a very personal subject, his sister, Nancy Gore Hunger, who had died of cancer in 1984. As he talked about his sister's courageous struggle to battle cancer, he voiced his concerns about the tobacco and smoking issue. His voice came to a low chatter, and his words became slow, as he painfully recalled his sisters struggle. Before his speech was over, hundreds of delegates were crying. He ended his speech saying that he would do everything in his power to make sure that others would not have to suffer the same fate as his beloved Nancy.

While there is no question that Gore was speaking from his heart and being sincere, the speech created some controversy, especially from his critics who said that he had overplayed the story to emotionally charge the crowd. They also charged that Gore had grown tobacco on his farm for many years and supported the tobacco industry while he was in Congress. But in reality, Al Gore was just showing his real side. His position on the tobacco issue had evolved since Nancy's cancer. And had he not felt in his heart this was what Nancy would have wanted him to do, then he would not have used her story in his convention speech. Gore is a man that is above everything loyal. And there has not been anyone more loyal to his family and close friends than Al Gore. Gore would later recount that he was surprised at the response of some of his critics. "I spoke publicly about my sister's death for the very first time, and was surprised that some felt the remarks were mawkish. Nancy played too important a role in my life not to talk about her at a moment when the nation was in the midst of a struggle with the tobacco companies to get them to change their ways and stop convincing young men and women to make the same deadly mistake Nancy had made when she started smoking at 13." "I also wish my family had extricated itself from growing tobacco sooner than it did after Nancy's illness. "Truthfully we all were numb during the onslaught of the cancer, and then our attention was focused on getting her well." "The implications of continuing to grow a crop on my father's farm that helped produce the cigarettes that had caused her fatal disease seemed a little abstract and a little remote at that point—in the same way that global warming seems remote to many now," Gore said.

Across the land, from the mountains of West Virginia to the coast of Oregon, the American people were going to the polls. Slowly, as the hours went by, millions of voters had already cast their ballots before Vice President Gore held his first meeting. By mid-afternoon, the Clinton campaign's private polls were showing that the president would win by a wide margin in both the popular vote and the Electoral College. Then it was finally over. President Clinton and Vice President Gore won re-election in a landslide over Senator Bob Dole and Jack Kemp. It was not even close. In the popular vote, President Clinton outpolled Senator Dole by 47,401,185 votes to 39,197,469, a margin over 8.2 million votes. Ross Perot managed to pull in 8,085,294 votes, almost half of what he tallied in 1992. The Electoral College map did not change much from the previous election, with the Clinton–Gore ticket winning 379 votes to the Republican ticket's 159. President Clinton was able to pick off several border south states (Arkansas, Tennessee, North Carolina, and West Virginia) in addition to Florida and Colorado. Clinton once again showed his rare ability to win in Republican-leaning states and win the majority of the Independent voters, including white males. He also carried women voters by almost 2 to 1. It was a very convincing victory for Clinton and Gore. The American people had spoken very clearly. They were happy with the direction of the country and the leadership of President Clinton and Vice President Gore. Life was very good for Clinton and Gore on election night in 1996. And the future could not have looked brighter.

During his eight years as Vice President, Al Gore, as time allowed, traveled back home to Tennessee. Typically he and his family would visit several times each year, ending the year with a two-week Christmas vacation, normally spent at the Gore's home in Carthage. The vice president would always fly into the Nashville National Guard airport. I had the opportunity to meet him several times when he traveled back to Tennessee. Having worked for him as an intern while he was in Congress, I kept in touch with him, and volunteered to work as staff assistant in his motorcade during his trips back to Tennessee. It was an exciting experience to participate in the vice-presidential motorcades. One such visit occurred on December 23, 1996. Karen Garner, one of Vice President Gore's staff volunteers, was in charge of the volunteer ground support. She and I drove up to the airport at the National Guard armory several hours before the vice president was scheduled to arrive. The vice president and his family arrived in Nashville at approximately 12:10 p.m. We were then instructed by the Secret Service to drive one of the vans that were parked beside *Air Force Two*. After I parked the van, I proceeded to assist the other staff volunteers and Secret Service with luggage and Christmas packages. Suddenly, the vice president emerged from *Air Force Two* and spotted me. He immediately came over to greet us, thanking us for helping out and asking how my family was doing. He never failed to always ask about my family, who had been involved in all his political campaigns since day one. His kindness and loyalty always struck me as rare for a politician.

We continued to load luggage and Christmas presents into the cargo vans. The van that I drove contained the Gore's Christmas presents, all neatly wrapped up in packages big and small. As I was driving in the motorcade I thought how neat it was to be delivering the vice president's Christmas presents. As the motorcade abruptly pulled out, there were seven or eight Tennessee Highway Patrol cars, four or five metro Nashville police cars, a slew of metro police motorcycles, and Secret Service SUVs. As we sped out of the airport, the police cars escorted the motorcade, with every exit and entrance along the interstate blocked by police. It was approximately a forty-five-minute drive from Nashville to Carthage along interstate I-40 East, a stretch of landscape made up of rolling hills and green pastures, separated by farms and a few small stores along the way. It is sparsely populated with a few small towns in between.

After the motorcade arrived in Carthage, the Secret Service and police vehicles drove up to the guarded gates that formed the perimeter of the vice president's farm house. From there we drove up to the vice president's house, which was located on a hill overlooking the valley and other neighboring farms, were populated with cattle and horses. The vice president and his family exited their limousine and proceeded into their house. After a few minutes, a Secret Service agent came up to the window of our van and instructed me to drive up behind the black unmarked Secret Service car that was parked in the driveway. Gore and his family then came outside the house, and we began to unload the luggage, gifts, and packages, handing them to the vice president and his family, as they each took turns taking items from our hands. It struck me odd that they picked up their own luggage and gifts, and I suddenly wondered if any other vice president had ever behaved this ordinary. After the vans were unpacked and the Gore's had taken their belongings inside their house, they came back out and got into the Secret Service car that was directly behind our vehicle. A secret service agent then came up beside my window and instructed me to drive behind the unmarked black vehicle. We drove by the house and down the long driveway and outside the guarded gate. Then we proceeded up the hill to his parent's house, where we spent another fifteen minutes unloading more Christmas packages. The vice president thanked us for all our help, and then he and his family went inside to enjoy another family Christmas. It was a very nice Christmas that year.[85]

---

85 Personal Letters from Author Troy Gipson.

CHAPTER 10

Gore Vice Presidency: 1997–2000

Vice President Gore, like all great leaders, is very complex. There are no sentences or paragraphs that can sum up this man. One only has to view his library that he maintained in his private residence at the Naval Mansion, which houses the Vice President. "A naval observatory clock read out of finial time in red digits to the hundredth of a second. In the corner stands a Nashville-style guitar, signed by country music greats. The bookshelves are full of popular works of history and politics and a massive, leather-bound Family Religious Reference. The profusion of photos are all-in-the-family. The four kids, Gore's parents, most of all Gore's wife, Tipper: the two of them as wooing youths, young parents, a mature couple."[86] This view into Gore's library of books and personal artifacts says more about the man than a thousand words could. He is a religious man but keeps his faith to himself. He is a public figure but really a private man. He is

---

86 Howard Fineman, *Newsweek*, May 24, 1999.

a man who is both proud of his heritage and roots, but also someone who is comfortable being a heartbeat away from the presidency.

During the second Clinton term, Gore continued to work extremely hard as vice president. President Clinton began to give him even more responsibilities and assignments, and Gore's work schedule became even crazier. Indeed, President Clinton would delegate more responsibility to Gore than any other Vice President in history. One of Clinton's former political advisors, Dick Morris, summed up Gore's enormous resume of responsibilities better than anyone has ever framed it during a 1998 interview with The New York Times Magazine.

"Areas where Al Gore makes the decisions---and the President rubberstamps--are science, technology, NASA, telecommunications, the environment, family leave, tobacco, nuclear dealings with the Russians, media violence, the Internet, privacy issues, and of course, reinventing Government. That's about a third of the Administration", Morris said.[87]

To accomplish the enormous amount of responsibilities given to him, Gore and his staff took careful planning. Gore was always very focused and disciplined, and went about his tasks devouring all available information and breaking it down into pieces he can hold in his hand and turn over in his mind", giving him the reputation as a policy wonk and intellectual. He would spend a typical morning or afternoon in meetings with Administration officials, Congressional leaders, Democratic Party officials, and private citizens. He would devour more than fifteen newspapers each morning. And in between reading he would snip out articles and tidbits of information and then place them into a neat folder. Then he would highlight the key points by paragraph and then by sentence until he had summed up the gist of the information. He would then typically give the pieces of paper to one of his aides and tell them that he wanted to schedule some time to meet with them on that issue. [88]

In early January of 1997, the Clinton–Gore administration received another economic boost, when the "American-led

---

87 Richard L. Burke, *New York Times Magazine*, February 22, 1998
88 Eric Pooley and Karen Tumulty, *Time*, December 15, 1997.

negotiations in Geneva produced an agreement to liberalize world trade in telecommunications services, opening 90 percent of the markets to U.S. firms. The negotiations were launched by Al Gore and conducted by Charlene Barshefsky. Their work was certain to bring new jobs and services at lower prices to Americans, and to spread the benefits of new technologies across the world."[89]

Then there was the extensive traveling as vice president representing the president and nation. There were hundreds of these trips during his eight years in office. And they were not just the "funeral" variety. They were legitimate trips that Gore took on behalf of President Clinton in order to help shore up foreign policy or campaign for Democrats running for election or re-election.

He flew to Japan for an international meeting on the Kyoto International Environmental Summit, where 160 nations gathered to discuss the effects of global warming and to adopt international laws to enforce the increasing threats to the environment. The vice president represented the United States at the summit and was instrumental in helping the countries reach a consensus on global warming and climate change. The agreement called for the United States to cut and reduce carbon emissions dramatically by 2010, with Europe and Japan also agreeing to further reductions. But the agreements that were reached at Kyoto were difficult. Vice President Gore toiled on the issue for many days before finally reaching a compromise with some of the nations that were holding out. There were both liberal and conservative critics. However, without Gore, the Clinton administration would not have been able to reach a meaningful agreement.[90]

At another trip across Texas, Gore met with reporters after a long three-day tour of the state. While flying back on *Air Force Two*, the vice president allowed a rare glimpse of his personal side, a side that few people get to know. "Around midnight after a three-city tour of Texas, the Vice President came wandering back to the press compartment of *Air Force Two*. Sliding in behind a table with the two reporters covering him that day, he picked slices of fruit from their

---

89 Bill Clinton, *My Life* (2004), 745–746.
90 *Tennessean*, December 14, 1997.

plates and spent two hours swapping opinions about movies and telling stories about old chums like Erich Segal, who, Gore said, used Al and Tipper as models for the uptight preppy and his free-spirited girlfriend in Love Story; and Gore's Harvard roommate Tommy Lee Jones", the famous movie actor." Then he moved on, grabbing a cocktail napkin to diagram a new system for making Internet connections via satellite. Through it all, he never let anything slip or allowed the conversation to turn back to the job. When he praised a PBS documentary on Harry Truman, a reporter observed that as VP, Truman rarely saw F.D.R. Gore changed the subject. And when the other correspondent asked him about the state of Clinton's second term, he rolled his eyes and moaned, "Don't make me work."[91]

There were stark differences between Clinton and Gore's political skills. Many people who worked for both stated that Gore was more "more resolute, more disciplined, and by far the better negotiator." "Bill Clinton would go into a room "wanting to make everyone like him," while Gore would go into a room wanting to "convince everyone he was right." Gore understood his adversaries, while Clinton would sometimes try to compromise too quickly. President Clinton would also explode with anger at his aides when he didn't get a clear answer or like the outcome. Al Gore, on the other hand, showed less anger, but he could also bristle when an aide or reporter challenged him directly.[92] There were also slight differences in the political philosophy of Clinton and Gore. Gore was "usually to the right of Clinton" on political issues. "He pressed Clinton to sign the welfare reform bill when the President seemed uncertain, for example, and argued for fiscal discipline before the President embraced full-fledged deficit reduction. Gore was also more hawkish on national defense issues than the President was. Even President Clinton himself stated that "When we went into Haiti, when we went into Bosnia, when 80 percent of the people in a poll said we shouldn't help Mexico and we helped Mexico, he was always on the strong side". [93]

---

91 *Time*, December 15, 1997.

92 Eric Pooley and Karen Tumulty, *Time*, December 15, 1997.

93 Richard L. Burke, *The New York Times Magazine*, February 22, 1998

The second term for Clinton and Gore was proceeding very smoothly. Then in January of 1998, all hell broke loose. The national media began to report that President Clinton had been accused of having an affair with a former intern. The accuser was a twenty-two-year-old lady named Monica Lewinsky, a former White House intern. All of Washington and the rest of the nation had come to a halt. The White House was now in the midst of the biggest scandal since Watergate. For Vice President Gore, the news was devastating. While he publicly supported the president and was careful in his assessment of the scandal, privately he felt betrayed, like most Americans.

As more information began to surface, it became clear that the allegations involving President Clinton and Monica Lewinsky, a former White House intern, were in fact true. The Lewinsky scandal would consume President Clinton and the White House for the next year, with an intense and unrelenting atmosphere of crisis hovering over the White House. An independent investigation was initiated into the events surrounding the scandal, which would eventually turn into a political witch hunt for the Republicans, end up costing the taxpayers millions of dollars and an enormous amount of political capital for Clinton and Gore. It would also rupture the personal friendship between President Clinton and Vice President Gore. Finally, after many months of investigation, and testimony before a federal grand jury, the scandal came to an end. The House of Representatives voted to impeach President Clinton on the charges of perjury and obstruction of justice. The United States Senate, however, voted for acquittal on all impeachment charges, thereby ensuring that the president would remain in office. But the scandal had taken a toll on the president, his family, the American people, and Al Gore.

After the Monica Lewinsky affair went public in 1998, the relationship between Vice President Gore and President Clinton became tense and awkward. Gore was badly shaken and angry like the rest of the nation, and in private he was livid about the reckless behavior that the President had demonstrated. Indeed, there was no hiding the fact that the Vice President was upset with the President. But Al Gore also knew that he had to take the high ground, not letting the scandal weaken his working relationship with the President. After all he was Clinton's closest advisor, who had been given more responsibility as Vice President than any other occupant in history. He and Clinton had always maintained a complicated yet respectful relationship, and they would continue that same working relationship throughout the scandal. But while Gore could not distance himself from the President since he would be viewed as disloyal, he also had to carefully balance his loyalty, insulating himself from the scandal itself. Only days after the scandal went public, the Vice President introduced President Clinton to an audience in Champaign-Irbana, Illinois, showing his loyalty without commenting on the scandal itself. Gore went to the podium and with a raised voice declared "He is the President of the country. He's also my friend. And I want to ask you now, every single one of you, to join me in supporting him and standing by his side." Gore had carefully calibrated his words before making the introduction, yet he was able to accomplish this mission without seeming to defend the President for his actions. In fact Gore's public demeanor towards the President reassured the nation in many ways, and for the sake of the country and Gore's own political career, the two men had to continue their work. [94]

But the scandal had done considerable damage to the Clinton presidency, and the President would spend the next two years trying to recapture his footing and popularity. As time went by, the American people seemed to forgive the President. However, there was little doubt that the Clinton–Lewinsky scandal hurt Gore immensely in his political future.

The vice president took another personal blow on December 5, 1998, when his beloved father, Albert Gore Sr., died of lung cancer at age ninety-one. This was a very difficult time for the vice president and his family. Gore's father had made a profound impact upon Al Gore, and also the nation. He had served the US with distinction in a political career that spanned 38 years in Congress, helping lead the country from the aftermath of World War II into a new age of innovation and revolution. The nation

---

94 Richard L. Burke, *New York Times Magazine*, February 22, 1998

had lost a true American hero, and Gore's father would be deeply missed. For Gore, the next few months would prove to be difficult, and he suffered the grief and depression that normally coincides with losing a parent. But he finally got back on his feet soon and concentrated on working for the American people as hard as he could, while simultaneously keeping his eyes on the next prize—the presidency.

The vice president and his wife, Tipper, shared a common interest in issues affecting families, including health care, mental health, and Medicare. They hosted an annual forum called the "Family Issues Conference." The conferences were held annually throughout the country. They believed that "families should be seen as both a resource to be tapped and a treasure to be protected when it comes to public policy." In one of their annual conferences held at Vanderbilt University in June 1998, Tipper Gore explained their concerns: "We were all concerned about the breakdown of the family. "We thought....What can we do to be part of the solution? What can we do to start strengthening families?" Al Gore also stated, "Should we curse the darkness? Let's light a candle."[95] While they both agreed that part of the reason to focus on family issues was because of their own experiences with their children, they really believed in helping families and the poor and downtrodden in society. And they believed the best way to strengthen families in our society is to ensure that public policy is written so that the government is an ally instead of an obstacle. While the Gores both dedicated much of their time to helping families, they would not discuss Albert III's accident or other way in which their own lives contributed to the conference agenda. However, it was Tipper Gore who, later on in the 2000 campaign, announced that she had suffered from depression for many years after young Albert's accident.

Tipper Gore could be very protective of her husband and was very concerned about how the public perceived him. "Friends say she was outraged by the negative news coverage Al received for his role in

---

95 Susan Page, *USA Today*, June 22, 1998.

the campaign fund-raising controversy". But the public scrutiny of
the Gores was to be expected. Such is the nature of today's politics.[96]

There would be one negative during Gore's tenure as vice president, one that even threatened his accession as the Democratic presidential nominee in 2000. This was the infamous "fundraising scandal," which caught Gore up in a legal campaign finance scandal. The
crisis that developed was from a series of personal telephone calls
that he made from his office in the White House, where he solicited
numerous campaign contributions from donors across the country.
The issue involved whether Gore had violated the Pendleton Act of
1887, which made it a felony for any person to solicit political dona-
tions in a federal building.

Janet Reno, the US attorney general, was given responsibility for
"reviewing whether the vice president's fund-raising activities may
have been improper for such a high-ranking official. The inquiry
could have also led to the appointment of a special prosecutor,
something that Gore and his 2000 campaign team could only gasp
at the prospect of. The fact of the case was that during 1997 through
1999, Vice President Gore had made numerous phone calls from
the White House. Federal law stated that it was illegal for any government official to conduct personal business on federal property.
But for Gore and his legal team, the question was whether the law
applied to a high-ranking official like the Vice President, who is on
the job 24 hours a day, 365 days a week. Indeed the law seemed to
be unclear. Gore attacked the issue head on, and in a press conference he publicly stated that there was "no controlling legal authority." The media and Gore's opponents began to sense blood in the
water, and they attacked him mercilessly. The *New York Times* wrote
a scathing editorial, stating that Gore had many gifts, but they did
not seem to include candor when it comes to the business of politics.
"In a *Los Angeles Times* poll published shortly after the scandal broke,
34% of the American people reported a favorable impression of the
Vice President, compared to a 59% favorability rating for President
Clinton. The scandal, no matter how innocent, was really begin-

---

96 Ibid.

ning to hurt Al Gore in the polls and ultimately his eye on the 2000 Presidency.

Up until the controversial fund-raising revelations, Gore's political future seemed secure. This issue more than any other in his career required Al Gore to defend his actions. It also tested his skill and fortitude at handling a political crisis. Throughout his career he had never faced a more critical event. How he handled this situation could either elevate his image or sink his presidential aspirations. It was indeed the most perilous moment of his entire political career. As the scandal continued, there were charges that "Gore may have been more immersed in fund raising than he had acknowledged, as well as the disclosure of memorandums suggesting that Vice President Gore could have known and should have known that some of his solicitations from the White House were not permitted on federal property."[97] Even the White House weighed in on how the scandal was hurting Gore in the public arena. "One White House official close to Gore said that 'this thing is out of control, and it's really hurting him. Who likes to see a person you really respect go through this? There are human stories here." Finally, after months of investigation, Attorney General Reno announced that there was no evidence that Gore intentionally violated the law, and that she would not appoint a special prosecutor to investigate the incident further. While the Republicans were upset and livid with this decision, Gore was elated and relieved.

As the second Clinton term came to a close, Vice President Gore began to take on an even more prominent role in the administration. President Clinton made it perfectly clear that Al Gore was his heir apparent to succeed him, and he intended to help Gore anyway possible to ensure his election. Clinton also ensured that all his White House staff and political aides were one hundred percent behind Vice President Gore. And thus the President would provide Al with as many political opportunities as possible. Clinton allowed Gore to select Carol Browner as the new Environmental Protection Agency head, who had worked for Gore previously and was one of his most trusted environmental advisors. Gore also recommended

---

97 Larry Daughtrey, *Tennessean*, September 14, 1997.

that Andrew Cuomo become the next Housing Secretary, providing him with another important political appointment for a friend who could help Al immensely in the next election. [98]

In 1999, the vice president was instrumental in helping to revitalize poor communities through the federally subsidized empowerment communities and enterprise zones. Gore paved the way in helping to provide $32 million in grants to communities in order to help the cleanup and development of "brown fields," which were contaminated rural and intercity areas that could be cleaned up and revitalized.[99] He also worked on immigration reform, and helped to foster in a regulation that assured "legal immigrants that they and their families can enroll in Medicaid, and the new Children's Health Insurance Program."[100]Vice President Gore also worked hard for the minimum wage increase enacted under the administration in 1996, which raised the minimum wage from $4.25 an hour to $5.15 an hour. Ten million Americans received an increase in wages. The vice president was also assigned co-chairman of the special bilateral commission with the heads of state of Russia and the Ukraine. It was on this commission in which Vice President Gore was instrumental in persuading Ukrainian President Leonid Kravchuck to hand over to Russia nuclear missiles, which had once been under Soviet control. He also negotiated with Russian Prime Minister Viktor Chernomyrdin in expanding Soviet trade with the United States. Al Gore had left an indelible mark on the Vice Presidency with his hands on advice and decisions in almost a third of the Federal Government, contributing an enormous amount of influence in President Clinton's legislative accomplishments. Indeed, Gore had played the greatest role ever by any Vice President before him. By the end of the Clinton Presidency there was no one better prepared to carry on the responsibilities of president than Al Gore

---

98 Richard L. Burke, *The New York Times Magazine*, February 22, 1998
99 Mimi Hall, *USA Today*, May 26, 1999.
100 Ibid.

CHAPTER 11

2000 Presidential Election

After serving as President Clinton's loyal vice president for eight years, it was finally time for Gore to take the reins as president of the United States. Everything had been set up almost perfectly for Gore to assume that office. The national economy was in great shape and the nation was at peace. Thus it was troubling to the vice president and his campaign team that he was still trailing in public opinion polls. Vice President Gore had also fought off a Democratic primary challenge from former Senator Bill Bradley (D-New York), whose candidacy created more headaches. The primary challenge forced the Gore campaign to spend valuable time and money in a primary fight that seemed to be unnecessary. And there were many in the Democratic Party who were not happy with Senator Bradley for challenging Gore, however liberal his cause may have been. Indeed it was a time that the Democrats didn't need a fight. It was a time to be united behind a loyal vice president who had accomplished so much for the nation and party, but politics is a hard life. Gore and his campaign team began to assemble a game plan they hoped would turn the tide. In an attempt to distance himself from President Clinton and the Lewinsky scandal, Al Gore decided early on to run his own campaign, on his terms. He was particularly sensitive to having President Clinton out making stump speeches, and decided not to ask the president to publicly campaign on his behalf. When asked "what role he envisioned" for the president, Gore replied, "He's got a full-time job being President and he's doing it extremely well." It was a pointed reply that summed up Gore's thinking.[101]

The vice president had a very experienced campaign staff, with most of them known as Washington insiders. He named Ron Klain, his chief of staff in the vice president's office, as his top political campaign advisor, and Donna Brazile as his Campaign Manager. Klain and Brazile were experienced and well liked by most Washington insiders. Gore also relied on some of his longtime aides who had worked for him since he was elected senator, and received advice from Tipper and his oldest daughter Karena. But in January of 2000, Al lost one of his closest political advisers, the talented Bob Squirer, who died of cancer.

The Republican Party, meanwhile, had all but anointed Texas Governor George W. Bush as its nominee, even though he still faced a serious challenge from Senator John McCain of Arizona. But the Texas governor had most of the National Republican Party establishment behind him, and of course his famous name didn't hurt his chances either.

George W. Bush, like Al Gore, was born into a powerful political family. His father, of course, was former President George H.W. Bush, and his grandfather, Prescott Bush, was also a powerful United States Senator from Connecticut, from 1952 to 1963. But unlike his father and grandfather, G.W. Bush grew up in Texas, and everything about him was Texan, from his talk to his walk. He was, by most accounts, likable and funny, but also brash and shrewd. While not an intellectual, like Gore, Bush was smart enough to graduate from Yale with decent grades. Bush had also managed to make a small fortune from the oil business, and, with the help of his father, as part owner of the Texas Rangers baseball club. He had sold his share of

---

101 Howard Fineman, *Time*, May 24, 1999, 44.

the Rangers in the early 1990s, reaping several million dollars of profit from a rather small initial investment. Bush also had been an effective Governor in Texas, even managing to work well with most Democrats in the state legislature. National Republican Party leaders had wooed him into running for president, partly because of his last name, but also because they considered him to be capable, likable, and, most importantly, electable.

While both Bush and Gore had been raised in a life among the powerful, and had both graduated from elite Ivy League schools, the comparisons ended there. Al Gore, unlike George Bush, was much more serious-minded and interested in complicated ideas and issues. He was likable, and could be funny and charming when he wanted to be, but he was not as natural at the good ole boy politicking like Bush. But Al Gore and George Bush both had a few things in common: they were both extremely loyal and determined, and really good family oriented men. They just happened to have a very different view of the role that the Government played.

After securing the Republican nomination, George Bush and his campaign turned their attention to Vice President Gore and the fall campaign. The Texas Governor, by most accounts, could not come close to matching Gore's impressive resume of public service. However, he had managed to maintain a lead over Gore in the national polls for the last year, and as he readied himself to take on Gore, he found himself in a good position. The national media and the Bush campaign began to frame Gore as a politician who changed his opinion based on convenience. They even made a big deal out of how he dressed and how stiff he could appear when making a speech. The national media also demonstrated an almost "overly aggressive" approach to covering Al Gore during his campaign, with many reporters focusing on the technicalities of Gore's comments or speeches, taking what he said out of context on many occasions. Indeed it appeared that many of the national media reporters and political pundits were trying their best to make Vice President Gore look like he was exaggerating the facts. In fairness though, the national media also portrayed George W. Bush to be inexperienced and lacking in qualifications. Many reported that he did not demonstrate a grasp of the issues, with some insinuating that the Texas governor did not have the intellect to be president. If the presidency had been won or lost on experience and qualifications alone, then Gore would have won in a landslide. But presidential elections are won or lost by a multitude of variables, and while the national media coverage was having an impact upon the race, it was only one aspect.

The election itself would prove to be won or lost by the candidates and their political campaigns. In Carl Rove, Governor Bush had one of the brightest and most ruthless of all campaign managers. Gore did not have anyone in his campaign that could match him, and it was now time for Gore to hire his own gunslingers and shake up his campaign. Finally, after many months of a stalled campaign, Al Gore made changes at the top and within the entire campaign organization. He hired a new campaign manager, Tony Coelho, the former congressman from California, to be his new campaign chairman, while moving Ron Klain to a lower-ranking position. Gore also moved his national campaign headquarters from Washington D.C. to Nashville, Tennessee, bringing along his entire campaign staff. Since he was still trailing in the public opinion polls, Gore would need to make a bold statement with his selection of a vice-presidential running mate. Speculation had been made that the vice president had narrowed his list to four or five potential candidates. They were Senators John Kerry, of Massachusetts; Evan Bayh, of Indiana; John Edwards, of North Carolina; and Senator Joe Lieberman, of Connecticut, who was seen as a long shot. The political odds makers seemed to believe that Gore would select either Edwards or Kerry. But to the surprise of almost everyone, the vice president selected Senator Joe Lieberman, of Connecticut. The selection of Lieberman was carefully calculated by Gore and his campaign managers. With Lieberman, Gore was getting someone that was very religious, with strong morals and character, while also helping in the important Jewish community. It also sent a message to the voters that a Gore White House would be much more sensitive to character and morality. Gore formally introduced Lieberman at a campaign rally in downtown Nashville on Tuesday, August 18.[102]

---

102 Eric Pooley, *Time*, August 21, 2000, 28.

By selecting Lieberman, the first Jewish candidate on a national ticket, Gore was taking a calculated risk and showing that he could make the tough decisions. While he would definitely help in the Jewish community, the question remained what effect it would have on non-Jewish voters. In the final analysis, the selection would prove to be very popular. It showed that he was not listening to the polls or making the decision based on politics. This resonated very well with Independent voters, and the race for the White House began to tighten. As the campaign finally began to click on all cylinders, Tony Coelho abruptly announced he was stepping down as campaign chairman due to medical reasons. Gore had to make a quick hire to replace Coelho, and he wasted little time by calling former Clinton Commerce Secretary William M. Daley, the eldest son of the famous Chicago Mayor Richard Daley, to be his new campaign chairman. Daley was just what Al Gore needed, a seasoned and skillful politician who had grown up in Chicago, a city noted for its tough politics. Daley made some changes within the campaign, bringing back Ron Klain, Gore's former chief of staff, to serve as one of the campaign's top operatives. While Daley was in charge of the campaign organization, Donna Brazile was the campaign manager, running the day-to-day operations. With the new campaign personnel now established, it was time for the Gore campaign to look toward the upcoming Democratic Convention in Los Angeles, California in August.

Forty years earlier, in the same city, at the same hotel, John F. Kennedy and his campaign entourage were in a hurry, frantically making their way through the lobby of the spacious Biltmore Hotel, on their way up to Suite 9333, where they would make their final and most critical decision of the campaign. The Biltmore, the crown jewel of Los Angeles, is "an enormous, tawdry, old-fashioned hostelry, which stands eleven stories high, dominating the green rectangle of Pershing Square, where the tired old men, the loafers, the time wasters and the free-speech enthusiasts make their permanent open-air headquarters of the Democratic National Committee."[103] Only a few days before Kennedy's arrival, Bobby Kennedy, his younger

---

103 Theodore White, *The Making of the President* (1960), 151.

brother and campaign adviser, was meeting privately with party delegates from many of the state delegations, but especially those of Texas, Illinois, California, Pennsylvania, and Minnesota. Finally, after several days of behind-the-scenes politicking, in smoke-filled rooms, the Kennedy campaign had finally secured enough delegates to win the Democratic nomination for president. Now Kennedy had himself arrived where he would meet his potential vice-presidential candidates, behind the scenes in the corridors and top-level suites of the Biltmore. Finally after several hours of debate and interviews, John F. Kennedy selected Lyndon Johnson to be his Vice Presidential running mate.

Now, forty years later, the Democrats had swooped into the same location and at the same hotel for its 2000 Democratic National Convention. For Vice President Gore, it would be the first opportunity to be on center stage after being in the president's shadow the last seven years. He would use the opportunity to advance his ideas before the American people, while also offering a contrast with his predecessor. It was the most critical time of the campaign, and Gore was prepared and determined.

As our plane landed at the Los Angeles International Airport, I looked out my window and there was *Air Force One*. President Clinton had flown into LA on the same Sunday afternoon that we arrived. Then later that night we saw the president's motorcade, as it raced down the streets of downtown LA, with dozens upon dozens of LAPD police cars surrounding the motorcade as it made its way to the downtown hotel.

Along with many other Gore friends and supporters, I attended the Democratic National Convention, staying at the famous Biltmore Hotel, which was the official Gore-Liebermann campaign headquarters, and also the location where many of the national delegates were gathered, including the Tennessee delegation. An intense excitement was reflected on the faces of the Gore delegates, friends, and supporters that filled the Biltmore Hotel lobby. The jingle and jangle of noise was everywhere, with screams of joy from the women and men who were now gathered together. It was an exhilarating experience to be part of the convention and to witness the pomp and celebration.

For the next four days, the Democrats would deliberate and plan their campaign strategy before Vice President Gore was nominated. The first three days of the convention were used as a buildup to the final night. During the day, Gore spent most of his time attending fundraisers, meeting with Democratic Party officials, and holding private meetings with friends and supporters across the city. There was little time to relax, and the pace was even more hectic than usual. But it was a time to celebrate, and many of the Vice Presidents friends, including Betty Fraley, Karen Garner, and Roy Tipps, were all from the same county (Franklin) in Tennessee, and had been elected as Gore delegates to the national convention. Many of Al Gore's political friends also attended, including Senators Jim Sasser, Roy Herron, and Thelma Harper of Tennessee, Congressman Bart Gordon (D-Murfreesboro), Congressman Bob Clement, Congressman Jim Cooper (D-Nashville), and Jane Eskind (Nashville). They were all excited to be a part of history, each of them recalling the days when Al Gore was just the son of a famous senator. On Wednesday afternoon, we attended a private campaign event for the Tennessee delegation at the NBC Universal in Pasadena, where Al Gore and Joe Lieberman and their families mingled with friends and supporters, enjoying a relaxed and informal atmosphere.

On Wednesday night, President Clinton spoke to the convention. The president marched to the podium as the crowd burst out with applause and tears, then he nodded to the crowd after what seemed like five minutes of applause. In his speech, he outlined his administration's many accomplishments during the last eight years, and noted that the economy was on firm ground and the nation was at peace. He also applauded Vice President Gore's tenure during the last eight years, stating in a thunderous voice that "You gave me that chance to turn those ideals and values into action after I made one of the best decisions of my life asking Al Gore to be my partner." By the time he had left the stage, he had lit up the crowd. The president had now made his case for Al Gore.

On Thursday night it was time for Vice President Gore to make his case before the American people. He made a very passionate speech about how much he had helped the administration oversee an economy that had brought prosperity, and foreign policy that had given peace. He outlined what he would do as president, contrasting his ideas with that of his Republican opponent. Moreover, he let it be known that he was his own man, and that he differed from President Clinton, if only on morals. He made that loud and clear as he only mentioned President Clinton's name once. The vice president stated that "we're entering a new time, we're electing a new President, and I stand here tonight as my own man. I want you to know me for who I truly am. "I'm here to talk seriously about the issues. I believe people deserve to know specifically what a candidate proposes to do. I intend to tell you tonight. You ought to be able to know and then judge for yourself," he said. After he ended his speech, he put an explanation point to that point. As Tipper came on stage to greet him, Al immediately embraced her and gave her a kiss that will go down in the annals of political history. The kiss lasted several seconds, and the audience exploded with applause. This simple gesture of love between the couple demonstrated to the nation and world that Al Gore was very much different than the President, and signalled a new beginning. The expectations had been raised very high, but Gore had not disappointed. Gore's speech was widely praised as being effective at providing the American people with a different view of him, while also demonstrating that he had command of the issues and the qualifications to be president. The Democratic National Convention had ended on a very high note, with Al Gore showing that he was very capable of following the path that the Democrats needed to take, one that would hopefully lead to another Democrat in the White House. After the convention, Gore rose in the polls to pull within two or three points of Governor Bush. The convention had been a resounding success, and Al Gore had finally been able to stand on his own, as his own man.

The campaign now turned to the presidential debates, and the debates would be another opportunity for Vice President Gore to show the American people why he should be the next president of the United States. Since the vice president had gained a reputation as being a great debater, the expectations were raised very high for him. In essence, there was more pressure on Vice President Gore than George W. Bush, who was not regarded as a great orator or debater. The first debate was held on October 3rd at the University of Massachusetts, in Boston. As the debate got underway, both Gore and Bush were effective as they answered the opening questions from the moderator. As the debate continued, Vice President Gore clearly communicated his ideas and demonstrated his knowledge on the issues very effectively. Whereas Governor Bush generalized his answers more than Gore, and didn't come close to Gore on the foreign policy questions. However there were several instances during the debate where Vice President Gore made sighs and gestures toward the Texas Governor as he was speaking. After the debate, the national media and political pundits gave Gore unflattering reviews, criticizing him for his mannerisms. They also reported that Gore seemed "too stiff" and "programmed," while Governor Bush appeared to be more natural and likable. While the first debate was not Gore's best performance, even by his own standards, the fact remained that the vice president was clearly the most articulate and informed of the two candidates. But in politics, perception is reality, and since the national media and political pundits always frame the winners and losers of the debates, Gore came up short of expectations. By the second debate, the Gore campaign had decided to make changes in the vice president's approach and style. This change required him to be more natural and less abrasive. But this change only served to complicate things and placed undue pressure upon the vice president. In the second debate, Gore appeared to be off key most of the night and came across as unnatural and uncomfortable. Even the tone of his voice was lower, which only made things worse. Indeed he really wasn't himself, and his political handlers had done him a disservice. The second debate was considered to be a draw by the national media and political pundits, with both Governor Bush and Vice President Gore demonstrating their grasps of the issues, while agreeing with each other on many issues. However, in the last debate, Gore was clearly the winner; he articulated his views clearly, while also demonstrating his extensive knowledge of complex issues. He also was much more focused and natural, and finally seemed to put it all together. Governor Bush, meanwhile, was less articulate and didn't demonstrate his knowledge on the issues as he had in the previous debates. The debates were now over, and while many voters were split in their assessments of the candidates, it was difficult

to ignore reality. Al Gore was clearly the most experienced and qualified candidate.

As the campaign went into the fall, the Gore campaign continued to focus on domestic issues. Vice President Gore would refer to
the great strides that he and President Clinton had made in improving the economy, building up a record-setting budget surplus during
the last eight years. Gore also was opposed to any changes to Social
Security, something that Governor Bush had proposed during the
campaign. The vice president also talked about the need to improve
health care. Because domestic and foreign policy matters were very
stable, the vice president could talk about such issues as health care
and the environment.

Governor Bush, meanwhile, was forced to focus on the Clinton
scandals, and restoring "honor and dignity" to the White House.
Indeed it was the centerpiece of his campaign and the only strategy that he could use in light of the successful domestic and foreign
policy issues. But the Texas Governor would also try to convince
the voters that Social Security needed to be reformed to allow individuals to put their money into private accounts. This was met with
much controversy by most voters and experts. Bush also began to
accuse the Clinton–Gore administration of being weak on national
security, and cited the Somalia tragedy in 1993 as an example.

In return, Vice President Gore questioned Bush's fitness for the
job, pointing to gaffes made by Governor Bush in interviews and
speeches, and suggesting the Texas governor lacked the necessary
experience to be president. The Bush camp responded by citing a
few gaffes that Gore himself had made, like when he was taken out
of context for saying that he "invented the Internet." But in fact,
Gore was one of the first politicians of either party to talk about
the future benefits of the information superhighway, which is what
the Internet was called back then. However, the perceived inconsist-
encies were enough to allow the media and the Bush campaign to
assault Gore for exaggerating the facts.

As the campaign continued, it was apparent that the Clinton
sex scandal was having a negative impact on the race. While Vice
President Gore continued to tell the American people that they
were far better off than they had been under the former Republican

administration, the fact remained that Gore was still trailing in the polls—in spite of the fact that the nation was enjoying peace and prosperity. The negative campaign attacks by the Bush campaign against Gore were apparently working. The Bush campaign ran political ads saying that Gore would take away their guns and was a big spending liberal who was out of touch with most Americans. But this was misleading, since Gore was considered a moderate while he was in Congress, and the legislation that he had supported addressing populist issues was extremely popular with the majority of Tennesseans, as well as the American people. He also had been a strong proponent for national defense, and during his service as vice president for eight years, Gore had helped President Clinton implement many moderate and conservative legislative initiatives, such as NAFTA, Welfare Reform, and the Reinventing Government initiative, which had helped save billions of federal dollars.

After a long and hard fought campaign, it was now time for the voters to decide. Leading up to the final weekend, the Gore campaign was receiving good news in the polls. Their private polling indicated that the race was tightening and that it would be much closer than what the political experts were predicting. On election night, both campaigns were nervous and anxious. It was now time to watch and wait. Slowly, as the hours went by, millions of voters had cast their ballots for president. As the results began to trickle in, Gore was performing extremely well in the New England states and in some of the Midwest. The race was very close in Iowa and Wisconsin, but the vice president was looking good in the large industrial belt states of Illinois, Michigan, and Pennsylvania. Bush, meanwhile, was sweeping the southern states, and he was performing well in the rural areas of the Midwest and was leading Gore in Missouri, Indiana, and Ohio. George Bush was also winning in Gore's home state of Tennessee by a small margin, and the outcome was likely to be close. Everything so far was expected, and all eyes began to turn to the bellwether state of Florida. Many people predicted that whichever candidate carried Florida would be elected President.

At approximately 7:50 p.m. (EST), the national television networks made what will forever be described as the biggest blunder in the history of televised elections. CBS News was the first network to declare Gore the winner in the state of Florida. This call sent shock waves throughout the country, especially to Governor George W. Bush, his family, and his top campaign operatives, Carl Rove and Karen Hughes. The governor was with his family watching the returns when he heard the news. There was hushed silence and disbelief. While the early exit polling results had been showing a very close race all day long, no one ever sensed that Florida could ever be lost. Then it was CNN's turn to declare Al Gore the winner in Florida, reaffirming the idea that maybe it was possible that Bush could actually lose the state. And if Florida went with Gore, then it was going to be a very long night for George W. Bush.

By this time the network analysts and political pundits knew an upset was at hand. Because the state of Florida was the cornerstone of the Bush electoral strategy, and since his brother Jeb was the governor there, it had been a foregone conclusion that its twenty-five electoral votes were firmly in Bush's hands. Without Florida, however, George Bush would be in an uphill battle the rest of the night. Shortly after Florida was called for Al Gore, CBS, CNN, and NBC called Michigan and Pennsylvania for Gore. Now it looked like a landslide in the making for Vice President Gore. But this would turn out to be a night in which all the conventional wisdom would be driven out the door. The drama was only beginning.

"At 9:55 p.m., CNN took Florida back from Al Gore, and put it into the category of "too close to call." The rest of the networks shortly followed. "By 1:30 a.m. most states had tumbled one way or the other, and both men had a total of 242 electoral votes. The counts were unimaginably, unbelievably close. Florida was still undecided, but by 2:30 a.m., the Texas Governor had built up a lead over Gore by more than 100,000 votes, with 85% of the votes counted. Now the television networks were ready to make another prediction. At approximately 2:35 a.m. est, the television networks declared George Bush the winner in Florida, and the next President of the United States.[104]

---

104 *Time*, November 20, 2000.

Gore and his family were stunned. His campaign chairman, Bill Daley, was pale. Everyone was in shock. Al consoled and comforted his family, and then he began to set in motion his concession speech. All the while, many of his top aides were urging him to wait a little longer before conceding. Tipper and Karena were begging him to hold off. But he was determined to get it over with. Gore then telephoned Governor Bush around 2:30 a.m. and conceded. Bush told Gore that he knew this was very difficult and said, "You are a good man".

Then over the course of the next hour, things changed again. Gore campaign aides, Senator Liebermann, and Al Gore himself began to receive desperate phone calls from supporters in Florida, telling them that the margin of votes in Florida was tumbling down into the hundreds. At one point the margin was 500 votes for Bush. Vice President Gore was already in his limousine, in a motorcade headed toward the War Memorial Building in downtown Nashville, where thousands of supporters had gathered. He would be making a concession speech to his supporters in only a few minutes. Then Bill Daley received a call from Gore campaign field director Michael Whouey, who told him to get in touch with the vice president. Daley was able to relay the message to the vice president just in time, just before he took the stage. Gore then huddled with his top campaign aides inside the offices at the War Memorial Building. At around 3:45 a.m., Vice President Gore picked up the phone and called Governor Bush again. He told the governor, "As you may know things have changed. The state of Florida is too close to call." Bush didn't take the news very well, and said, "Let me make sure I understand. You're calling me back to retract your concession." Gore replied, "Well there's no reason to get snippy. Bush then told Gore that his brother Jeb was in the room and had assured him that he had enough votes to win in Florida. Gore replied, "Let me explain it to you. Your brother is not the ultimate authority in this matter." And with that, Governor Bush said, "Well Mr. Vice President you need to do what you have to do."[105]

---

105 Ibid.

The election was not over, and had suddenly taken an unexpected turn. Indeed it was so close that neither Bush nor Gore knew what the outcome would be. As the final national results were tallied, Governor Bush had won 246 electoral votes, while Al Gore had won 255 votes; 270 votes were needed to win. Meanwhile, two smaller states, New Mexico, with five electoral votes, and Oregon, with seven electoral votes, were still too close to call. But Florida, with its twenty-five electoral votes, was the focus of attention as the morning hours began to trickle by. As the final precincts in the Florida counties reported their voting results to the Florida Election Commission, the official tally showed Governor Bush with a 1,784 vote lead over Vice President Gore. The television networks continued their election coverage, as the American people went to bed confused and uncertain.

CHAPTER 12

Supreme Injustice

The American people awoke on Wednesday morning not knowing who the new leader of the free world would be. Not only was it unclear who would be the next president, it was also uncertain how the nation could be governed by either Gore or Bush, in light of the election controversy and the division of the nation. By Florida state law, since the final vote margin was less than one-half percent, an automatic recount of all the votes was required. This meant that Governor Bush's current small lead, and the final outcome of the presidential election, now depended on the recounting of votes.

In the aftermath of the election, both Gore and Bush prepared for another battle, a legal contest that would be waged to try and determine if all the votes in Florida had been counted. It would be a contest which would be fought as equally hard as the campaign leading up to the election. Both campaigns prepared by sending hundreds of lawyers down to Florida, putting them on the ground floor with the election officials, party operatives, and the voters themselves. It would turn out to be a thirty-six-day exercise akin to poker, only the odds were more difficult to predict. The Bush campaign turned to former Secretary of State James Baker to head up his legal team, while Gore chose former Secretary of State Warren Christopher as his top legal adviser. The difficult part for Vice President Gore would be to show the American people that he had a viable case for the recount while running against time. If the public became impatient with the process, his legitimacy would be lost and thus his hopes for victory. However, it became clear to the entire nation that the Florida voting had been flawed in many ways: thousands of votes had been rejected by voting machines; thousands of voters' names had been purged from the voting rolls; even some of the ballots were odd and confusing. In Palm Beach County, an affluent area made up of many Jewish retirees, the voting ballots became the issue. Patrick Buchanan, the Reform Party candidate, had amassed nearly 3,407 votes in the heavily Democratic community, which led many people to question the results, wondering how Buchanan, not exactly a friend of many Jewish voters, could amass that many votes. Early on the morning of the election, Gore's top campaign aides began receiving frantic phone calls from Democratic supporters and campaign operatives in Florida, saying that there were ballots in Palm Beach County that were confusing the voters. After the election, it was discovered that the so-called butterfly ballots had been printed in a way that caused great confusion to the voters. George Bush's name was listed first, on the left side of the ballot, with a "punch hole" next to his name. Al Gore's name was listed next, directly below Bush's name. Patrick Buchanan's name was on the right hand side of the ballot directly across from Bush and Gore, with his punch hole listed between the two. However, when a voter punched the hole next to Gore's name, the result was actually Patrick Buchanan's name across from that of Vice President Gore. And while there were little arrows that were designed to direct the voters to the appropriate hole for their candidate, there were still many voters who were confused. To make matters even worse, Florida did not allow voters to cast "provisional" ballots, so if there was an error made, the voters could only complain. While it had been a registered Democrat who had ordered the printing of the "butterfly ballots," this did little to console the Gore campaign. It was indeed one of the most bizarre incidents of the entire election fiasco, leaving one to wonder how a "butterfly ballot" could be approved as method for casting ballot. On Thursday, November 9, however, the mechanical recounts in the state of Florida showed Governor Bush leading Gore by only 327 votes. The margin had dwindled even further, which served to reenergize Gore and his campaign.[106]

There were four counties in southern Florida that the Gore campaign targeted (Broward, Miami Dade, Palm Beach, and Volusia), and all four of them were Democratic strongholds. Al Gore and his team, including William Daley and Warren Christopher, debated at length about what Gore's next move should be. It was finally decided that the campaign should petition the local parties in each of the counties to proceed with requesting manual recounts. On Thursday, November 9, the Gore campaign and the Democratic Party requested manual recounts in three counties (Broward, Palm Beach, and Miami Dade), as provided for under Florida state law. Since Florida state law did not specify how the vote recounts were to be conducted, this allowed both the Democrats and Republicans to interpret the rules differently, based on what would best satisfy their candidate. In the case of Al Gore's campaign, the broader the scope of the recounts the better, while George Bush and the Republicans preferred the smaller, less rigorous method and scope.[107] The Gore team was particularly interested in recounting all of the "punch card" ballots that were cast in Broward and Palm Beach counties, where thousands of votes had been rejected by voting machines. This was because many of the punch card ballots contained small paper flaps, or "chads," that were designed to be punched through. The problem was that if the voter left a paper flap hanging (a "hanging chad"), the voting machine might not recognize the punch as a vote, thus resulting in the vote being rejected. Gore and his legal team argued that if the ballot had an indentation, it meant the voter's intention was clear. Thus Gore's campaign calculated they could pick up a few thousand more votes by recounting the punch card ballots. This would prove to be controversial, and forced the Florida

---

106 Jeffrey Toobin, *Too Close to Call* (2001).
107 Ibid.

State Election Commission into not only recounting the vote totals, but also trying to determine what a voter's intent had been. Thus the contest for the presidency came down to the recounting of votes, and the possibility of a complete statewide recount of all votes that were cast, and now it was a race against time. The Bush campaign, meanwhile, also requested recounts in some of the Republican strongholds across the state, hoping to pick up additional votes that may not have been counted. In addition, Bush requested recounts of the overseas military absentee ballots, which they calculated would provide them with additional votes since the majority of those votes were from servicemen and veterans, who normally vote Republican.

However, just like the voting process in Florida, there were some problems with the overseas ballots. Gore's team quickly picked up on information received from Jacksonville, one of the largest military towns in Florida, that there were hundreds of overseas military ballots that were post marked after the deadline. Meanwhile, on Thanksgiving weekend, Gore was meeting with his legal team inside the vice president's mansion in Washington. There, in a meeting with his lawyer, David Boies, and campaign adviser, Ron Klain, the discussion turned to the legality of the military ballots. One of Gore's top advisers had calculated that without the additional military ballots, Bush's lead would likely evaporate and give Gore a small winning margin, possibly as low as nine votes. Ron Klain told the vice president, "We can win the election without any more counting in Miami and Palm Beach." "If you don't go after the military-ballot thing, you have to have counting, and that may take time," said Klain.[108] But Gore was not having any part of it, and he told his aides that he would not contest the ballots, stating, "Even accepting that Ron is right and there is a theoretical way that I could win by nine votes, I couldn't be president of the United States that way. It's not right. If we knock out thousands of military votes of military people, I couldn't govern. I could win, but I couldn't govern."[109] Gore had acted nobly and justly, demonstrating his greater commitment to his country above that of winning the presidency. After the overseas

---

108 Ibid.
109 Ibid

military ballots were counted, Bush's lead increased from 300 to 930 votes.

But there would continue to be much controversy over the recounts, and the Bush campaign was privately trying their best to halt the recounting. They found a friend and ally in Florida Secretary of State Katherine Harris, a Republican that had been appointed by Governor Jeb Bush. The Gore team was very concerned about the potential conflict of interest in the outcome of the election. Sure enough, as the weeks went by, the partisan politics began to take shape, and Secretary Harris announced that her office was opposed to any "hand recounts" and would also try to end the manual recounts very quickly.

So George Bush and his legal team went to work, trying to prevent anymore recounts. On November 11, Bush filed suit in a federal district court in Miami, requesting the court to stop the manual recounting. The district court spent the next day deliberating, before ruling on November 13, voting to reject Bush's request to stop the recounts. Then on the same day, the office of Secretary of State Katherine Harris released her legal opinion, stating that the deadline for the election certification would be November 14, with no manual recounts to be included or permitted. Yet the drama would continue, and the most bizarre presidential election in the last hundred years would become even more bizarre and unpredictable. The Gore team believed the decision by the secretary of state was unfair, and a blatant attempt by the Republican Party to ensure that George Bush would win in Florida. The Gore team then appealed the secretary's decision to a state district judge, who ruled that the secretary of state had not used sound judgment, and that the recounts should continue. Thus, the recounts continued on, and the patience of the American people began to wane.[110]

On Wednesday, November 16, Gore made a bold move. He decided to take his case to the American people. During a live nationally televised speech, Gore proposed to Governor Bush either a "hand recount" in the disputed Democratic counties, or a statewide recount by hand. Bush quickly declined the proposal.

---

110 Ibid.

The Bush team believed that both options benefited Vice President Gore, and they were unwilling to take any chances. In private the Bush campaign believed they were lucky to have carried Florida, realizing that the controversial ballots in several of the Democratic counties most likely cost Gore several thousand votes. Then on November 20, lawyers for both Bush and Gore went before the Florida Supreme Court to argue the issue of whether the hand counts should be included in the final results. After hearing the request, on November 21, the Florida Supreme Court ruled that the hand counts must be included, and also extended the recount deadline to November 26, allowing the recounting of some seventy thousand ballots to continue. The Gore campaign was ecstatic, but they knew this ruling would also be challenged in court by the Bush team. The recounts continued, with much controversy developing over the canvassing boards, and the process that was used to determine if a hanging chad was an actual vote. In some of the county precincts, demonstrations broke out. There was political maneuvering on both sides, and it reminded the nation once again just how divided the people were. Governor Bush and his team were now privately worried that he might actually lose the election after all. They believed that Vice President Gore and his team were trying to steal the election, and their time and patience had been completely exhausted. They were now ready to take the fight to another level. On November 22, the Bush team formally appealed the Florida Supreme Court's decision to the United States Supreme Court. The political and legal posturing had now made its way to the highest court in the nation. The election of the president was now in the hands of the US Supreme Court, and the case was a first for the United States.

Meanwhile, on November 26, Florida Secretary of State Katherine Harris proceeded on and certified George W. Bush the winner of Florida's 25 electorate votes, by 537 votes. The very next day, Vice President Gore and his legal team appealed the secretary's decision to the Florida Supreme Court, and on December 1, the Florida Supreme Court ruled in favor of Gore and immediately ordered the recounting of ballots that were previously rejected by the voting machines.

In what would later become known as *Bush vs. Gore*, the case went before the US Supreme Court on December 11, 2000, with the Supreme Court hearing both sides of the argument. David Boies was the lawyer who represented Al Gore, and he argued before the Court that the Florida Supreme Court had ruled in accordance with its normal statutory states' rights, and that it had not violated the US Constitution in doing so. Theodore Olson, the lawyer representing Bush, countered, saying that the Florida Supreme Court had erroneously ruled in such a way as to effectively make state law, therefore violating the US Constitution. Finally, on December 12, the Court ruled by a 7–2 vote that the Florida Supreme Court's ruling requiring a statewide recount of ballots was unconstitutional, because it violated the Equal Protection Clause under the US Constitution. The Supreme Court then voted on a separate measure in regard to the completion of the recounts, voting 5–4 to halt the Florida state recount, and mandated that the previously certified vote totals should stand. The five justices nominated by Republican presidents (Justices Rehnquist, Scalia, Thomas, Kennedy, and O'Connor) all voted against the recount, while the four remaining justices (Justices Stevens, Ginsberg, Souter, and Breyer) voted in favor of the recount. The decision was unsigned, and the ruling was deemed "limited to the present circumstances." The great irony of this decision is that the five justices who voted against Gore were all considered to be advocates of *judicial restraint*, which, by definition, is "a judicial interpretation that emphasizes the limited nature of the court's power, and asks judges to base their judicial decisions solely on the concept of *stare decisis*, which refers to an obligation of the court to honor previous decisions." The decision that the US Supreme Court made was one of the most politically motivated and ideologically divided in the history of the United States. In the nations history, never before has a more important decision been made by the US Supreme Court. Thus the US Supreme Court was divided like the rest of the American people, and with that swift decision, Gore's political career had ended, at least for now. Vice President Gore later commented on the Courts decision. "I was surprised because the philosophy that had been followed by the conservative majority on the court was completely inconsistent with a decision to take the case away from the state court. After the shock and surprise, I just shifted into trying to respond in the most effective way I could. I held out every hope that the court would do what I personally felt was the right thing, but I had tried to prepare both myself and my family for the eventuality that it would not come out our way....We had prayed together frequently as a family that we would not be vulnerable to bitterness. We tried to reach out for a higher plane"[111]Gore stated.

Shortly after the Supreme Court's decision, the vice president scheduled a speech to be delivered to a national television audience. On December 13, 2000, Al Gore made a formal concession speech before a live television and radio audience. He gave an eloquent speech outlining his patriotism and faith in the American democracy. He stated, "Now the Supreme Court has spoken. Let there be no doubt, while I strongly disagree with the Court's decision, I accept it. I accept the finality of this outcome which will be ratified next Monday in the Electoral College. And tonight, for the sake of our unity as a people and the strength of our democracy, I offer my concession." "This has been an extraordinary election. But in one of God's unforeseen paths this belatedly broken impasse can point us all to a new common ground, for its very closeness can serve to remind us that we are one people with a shared history and a shared destiny". "And now my friends, in a phrase I once addressed to others: it's time for me to go. Thank you and good night, and God bless America."[112]

Al Gore had just missed fulfilling his dream. The defeat was very bitter and unfair and had left Gore and his supporters feeling robbed. Indeed it was the cruelest ending possible to a presidential campaign that had managed to pull even and overtake Governor Bush in the popular vote. Though Gore came in second in the electoral vote, he received 543,895 more popular votes than Bush. But it was bittersweet and only gave more credence to the belief that Gore likely would have won Florida with a statewide recount. In fact, there were several independent surveys conducted in Florida after

111 The Washington Times Magazine, Nov. 17, 2002, by Lisa Mundy
112 Speech by Al Gore, December 13, 2000.

the election, with most all of them showing that the flawed voting, from the controversial butterfly ballots to the hanging chads, most likely cost Al Gore the Presidency. The Palm Beach Post conducted their own independent review of some "6,607 discarded votes when voters marked more than one name on the county's "butterfly ballot", and reported that "voters who marked Gore's name and that of another candidate totaled more than 10 times the winning margin Bush received to claim Florida's 25 electoral votes and the White House". They also found that of the "5,330" overvotes, "Palm Beach County residents invalidated their ballots by punching chads for Gore and Reform Party candidate Pat Buchannan was located just above Gore's on the two-page ballot".[113]

Ron Klain, Gore's campaign lead legal strategist stated that "What it shows is what we've been saying all along, there is no question that the majority of people on Election Day believed they left the booth voting for Al Gore".[114]

There were no shortages of Monday morning political quarterbacks giving their opinions on the narrow loss. Many Democrats and political pundits pointed out that if President Clinton, the great campaigner, had been allowed to go into some of the key toss-up states, the odds are that Gore would have won. But Vice President Gore disagreed, and stated in a 2002 interview that he didn't believe leaving President Clinton out of his campaign was one of his campaign's mistakes, "because President Clinton has said himself that all campaigns are about the future, not the past." "And I think that the popularity of one person very seldom is transferable to someone else. I think you have to go out there and present yourself and your own program and your own policies".[115]

The vice president also stated that he took full responsibility for the loss. "I think one of the things that I have learned from the Campaign is that it's always a mistake to hold back, in anyway, and

---

113 Palm Beach Post,

114 Ibid.

115 Al Gore, interview by Larry King, *Larry King Live*, CNN, November 19, 2002.

just let it rip out and let the chips fall were they may."[116]Gore also admitted that the American people didn't really get to see his other, more comfortable side during the campaign. He stated, "I think the older I get, the more comfortable I am in just letting my hair down in all settings. I come out of a political tradition in Middle Tennessee that my father was part of, that Cordell Hull before him was part of, that has a more formal public way. I think that was a failing of mine, sure."[117]

There were also many political experts who believed that Ralph Nader, the Green Party candidate, likely cost Gore at least two states (New Hampshire and Florida). And there is strong evidence to suggest Nader may have taken away more votes from Gore than he did from Bush. In New Hampshire, Bush beat Gore by only 7,211 votes, with Ralph Nader gaining 22,198 votes, and in Florida, Nader amassed a total of 97,488 votes. Many people believe that most of Nader's support would have gone to Vice President Gore, since the Green Party, and its political platform, is more similar to the Democratic Party than the Republican Party. Whether or not Ralph Nader served to be a spoiler will be debated for years to come. The Gore campaign had also calculated that they would win in Tennessee, speculating that the vice president would surely win the state, if only by a small margin. After all, the Clinton–Gore campaign had carried the Tennessee in both 1992 and 1996, thus there was little reason to believe that Gore wouldn't carry the state on his name alone. Moreover, it should have been enough to win it for him, given the fact that he had accomplished many good things for Tennessee and the country during his years in Congress and as vice president. The national media also marginalized and trivialized Gore, seeming to ignore the vast contributions that he had made while as Vice President and in Congress. And much of the American people seemed to take for granted the enormous peace and prosperity that the nation was experiencing. It was as if they falsely believed that the good times would continue on,

---

116 Ibid.
117 Ibid.

regardless of who was President. We now know that the election did matter, and that the man who took office in 2001 went on to lead the nation in a much different direction. Whatever the main reasons were, the hard truth was that Al Gore would not be president. He would have to spend the next few years trying to decide if he would run again, and only time would tell. But what no one could deny Gore was his place in history. For now he had ended a political career with many important and historic achievements, and could hold his head high.

CHAPTER 13

The Morning After

It was now time for Al Gore to turn the page to a new chapter in his life. The very moment he left the vice presidency he became a private citizen again. But he still had many things to reflect upon, and his future still looked bright. He was as determined as ever, and his desire was still there, but he was stunned and exhausted. The campaign and the cruel ending had taken a toll on him, scarring his spirit and soul. In the process he would experience bouts of anger and depression. It would take a long time for his wounds to heal. But Al Gore is very strong, and in the back of his mind he knew that his future was far from over. For now, though, he would try to focus on recovery, rest, and reflection.

As Gore reflected on the election, there was one painful reminder that would not go away. If only he had carried his home state of Tennessee, the Florida controversy would not have been an issue, and he would now be president. So he found himself digging deeply to try to understand how many of the voters in his own state could suddenly turn their backs on him after all the many good things he had done. But in his own way of looking at things, he didn't point fingers. He was more hurt than angry.

Instead of replaying the what-ifs, he would look to the future. Soon after he left the vice presidency, in January 2001, he and Tipper announced their plans to move back to Tennessee. Gore said he had "fences to mend" back in Tennessee. He was clearly thinking ahead and knew that if he ran for president again in 2004, he would have to spend more time in Tennessee, reconnecting with his old friends and colleagues. In essence, Al Gore was politely saying to his friends and supporters that he knew he should have won Tennessee and the election, and in hindsight he would have conducted his campaign differently. He was still holding out hope for another opportunity. Yet even Gore himself did not know if he would ever run for office again, and he would spend the next year and half undergoing a transformation of life. He was slowly but gradually beginning to heal.

In January 2001, Gore announced that he had accepted teaching positions with three universities (Middle Tennessee State University, Fisk University, and Columbia). In his new positions, he would act as a visiting professor at the universities, teaching courses in government. When asked if he was interested in running for president again, he remarked, "I'm not considering anything political right now, but I haven't ruled out thinking about such things later on." "The only decision I've made about politics is not to make a decision until I've had more time for reflection and rest."[118] His remarks further solidified the prospects of another presidential bid. And there were no shortage of avid supporters within the Democratic Party who wanted and expected him to run again.

In the spring of 2001, Al and Tipper took a trip to St. Thomas in the Caribbean, trying to get away and relax for a few days. There the Gore's were able to relax, spending their time reading and walking down the beach, with politics far from their minds. But the Vice President was still thinking about the aftermath of the election. During this transitional time, Gore stated that he was "simply trying to keep busy, to stay scheduled, almost as if

---

118 Kevin Sack, *New York Times*, January 25, 2001.

nothing had changed. I've always thrown myself into my work. I think it was a continuation of that pattern a little bit".[119] This was the way that Gore coped in dealing with the emotional pain from the election. Looking back at this period of time in Gore's life, friends say that he became isolated, cutting many of his old friends off, while staying in touch with only a few close friends. Then later on that summer, Al and Tipper took a six week vacation in Europe, visiting Spain, Italy and Greece. For the first time since the election, the couple were able to be alone and relax, not being under any pressure of a schedule. It also allowed Al to further reflect upon his life and future, allowing him to quietly re-evaluate is thoughts.

Al Gore's relationship with President Clinton was repaired somewhat just after the September 11, 2001, terrorist attacks. Gore was out of the country on one of his environmental campaign trips, giving a slide presentation, when the planes hit the World Trade Center. Upon hearing the tragic news, he phoned Tipper and his family members, relieved that they were all safe. But like the rest of the United States, and even the world, Al Gore was shocked and saddened. With flights to the United States halted, he found himself isolated, removed from the people of the United States. The vice president wanted to return home quickly to be with his family, and to join the rest of the nation's citizens in their grieving and united spirit. He finally was able to locate a flight into Canada, where upon arrival he was driven across the border into Buffalo, N.Y. by the Royal Canadian Police, and then he and an aide rented a car and proceeded to drive down into the United States. As he was traveling along in the car, President Bill Clinton telephoned him, having just arrived from Australia by a Military transport plane. The President greeted him warmly and graciously, telling him that President Bush was sending a Military Plane to take him to Washington for the national prayer service at the National Cathedral. Clinton also invited him down to his home in Chappaqua, N.Y., providing him directions on how to get to his house. The Vice President accepted, and drove his way down to New York, where he finally arrived at

---

119 Richard L. Berke, *New York Times Magazine*, February 22, 1998

around 3:30 a.m. As Gore approached Clinton' house, the President
was still awake waiting for him to arrive.[120]

President Clinton later described the event "Al arrives at about
3:30 in the morning, see's the refrigerator on the porch, and the
first thing he says is, "I see you've managed to bring a little bit of
Arkansas to New York", Clinton said. "And I knew that after all he'd
been through he hadn't lost his sense of humor". Gore and Clinton
then talked all night long, rekindling the close friendship that they
had experienced in the White House. The next day they boarded
the Military plane and flew into Washington, D.C. for the memorial
service at the National Cathedral, where they joined President Bush
and other political dignitaries in the solemn service.

Thus an unexpected national tragedy had united Bill Clinton and
Al Gore once again. Gore later stated, "There were tensions after
the campaign, partly because we had not been in as close personal
communication. We didn't talk regularly, so a backlog had been built
up. And I went in after the election and we kind of cleared the air a
little bit and tried to lay the framework, ground work for renewing
the close friendship we had. And that's succeeded."[121]

In 2002, Al and Tipper purchased an old colonial mansion in
the exclusive Bell Meade suburb of Nashville for $2.3 million. The
house, dating back to 1915, is white, with black-trimmed windows,
surrounded by iron gates. It is a graceful and dignified place, like
the old southern plantations that were formal, peaceful and gran-
deur, but it is also equipped with the world's latest technology. The
Gores later renovated and retrofitted the house with environmental
friendly features, including solar panels, geothermal heating, and a
state-of-the-art rain-collection system. The house included offices
for the Gores, in addition to a gym. It was the perfect fit for a man
who is distinguished and dignified, offering a place to live, work, and
entertain world celebrities.

As Al Gore was enjoying being a private citizen once again, he
was still looking ahead to 2004. He would spend the next two years

---

120 Ibid.

121 Al Gore, interview by Larry King, *Larry King Live*, CNN, November 19,
    2002.

trying to determine if he really wanted to go through another presidential election. Meanwhile, all of his political friends and most Democratic activists were urging him to run. His family was more divided on the idea, but they were still supportive in any decision that he would ultimately make. But it would take a long time before Al Gore could decide.

Shortly after he left the vice presidency, Al Gore announced that he would join Google as a senior adviser. In his new role, Gore would serve as a key adviser and analyst in helping the company develop and market its technology. The decision to work with Google would prove to be a cleaver and rewarding move for Al Gore. He could foresee Google's bright future in the scope of computer technology, and he would play a big role in helping Google become one of the leading companies in the world. He would also reap enormous benefits later as the company's stock increased dramatically, becoming one of the most valuable and widely held stocks in the world.

One day Steve Jobs, Apple Founder and CEO, called Al Gore. He spoke to him very warmly and asked if he would agree to serve on the Board of Directors of Apple Computer. Gore accepted the offer. Steve Jobs was overjoyed and released a statement lauding the former vice president: "Al brings an incredible wealth of knowledge and wisdom to Apple from having helped run the largest organization in the world—the United States government—as a Congressman, Senator and our 45th Vice President. Al is also an avid Mac user and does his own video editing in Final Cut Pro," said Steve Jobs, Apple's CEO. "Al is going to be a terrific Director and we're excited and honored that he has chosen Apple as his first private sector board to serve on." Apple Press Release, March 19, 2003. The feelings were mutual as Al Gore stated. "Steve and his team have done an incredible job in making Apple once again the very best in the world." "I have been particularly impressed with the new Mac OS X operating system and the company's commitment to the open source movement. And I am especially looking forward to working with and learning from the great board members who have guided this legendary company's inspiring resurgence."[122]Thus began a new chapter in the life of Al Gore. As a company director and board member of Apple, Gore was compensated through shares of common stock. Initially, Gore was given 30,000 shares, which were exercisable at $14.75 per share. At the time, Apple's stock was trading at approximately $21 per share. Eventually, however, the price of Apple stock would soar, finally topping out at over $700 per share in 2012. This, of course, would allow Gore the opportunity to exercise his shares for an enormous profit.

As time went by, Gore developed a very close friendship with Steve Jobs. They had many things in common, as both were technocrats who were intrigued by technology and innovation, and who also shared an interest in the environment. As a board member at Apple, Gore would offer great experience. He was business savvy by nature and was very interested in technology. During his years in Congress and as vice president, he had demonstrated his knowledge of technology, and was very skilled at understanding the complexities of such issues as computer technology and the structure of the Internet. Thus it was a natural fit for Gore to become a member of the Apple team. Gore would play a key role in helping to guide the company into the twenty-first century. Indeed he would prove to be one of Apple's most influential board members, and one of Steve Job's closest friends and advisers. The decision to serve on Apple's board would prove to be one of the smartest moves in Al Gore's life, and would allow him to increase his personal wealth substantially. He has done well for himself since leaving public service, and has been very successful as a business entrepreneur.

As the next presidential election approached, Al Gore was still trying to decide if he would be a candidate for president in 2004. The Democrats loved Gore, and if he chose to run again he would be the prohibitive favorite for his party's nomination. After almost two years of speculation on whether he would run again, he had finally made up his mind.

In early December of 2002, Gore was still trying to decide if he would be a candidate. He flew to New York City, where he spent several days deliberating on whether to make another run for the

---

122 Apple Press Release, March 19, 2003.

Presidency. He was also scheduled to appear on the Saturday Night Live Show that weekend and on the CBS network on Sunday evening. The suspense was building and Gore's friends and supporters believed that he would announce his decision to run. But on December 14, 2002, Gore announced that he would not be a candidate for resident in 2004. In an interview with *60 Minutes*, Gore stated, "I've decided that I will not be a candidate for President in 2004. I personally have the energy and drive and ambition to make another campaign, but I don't think it's the right thing for me to do."[123] "Because I have run for president twice before and because a race this time around will focus on a Bush–Gore rematch, I felt that the focus on that race would inevitably have been more on the past than it should've been when all races should be focused on the future," Gore said, the day after making his announcement. The news was met with shock and disbelief by Gore's staff, friends, and supporters. Gore's decision was made after much debate and deliberation. He knew that his prospects would be good and was convinced he could win, but he had lost his love of politics, and no longer felt the need to be president. He also seemed to be content with his current life, which included teaching, making speeches on the climate crisis, and working in the corporate world. For weeks leading up to the announcement, Gore had been saying that he would make a decision by the first of the year. Furthermore, he had given a number of television interviews and spoken at numerous Democratic Party events during the year. Thus he decided not to seek the presidency again, and instead would continue to focus on the climate crisis. It appeared that Al Gore's political career was finally over. But while his political career had apparently ended, his new career was just beginning to take off.

There would be another tragedy for Gore. His beloved mother, Pauline Gore, passed away on December 15, 2004, at the age of ninety-two, after a long illness from strokes and heart problems. It was another tough blow to Al. He stated that "she was my father's closest adviser. Together they strengthened the future of this great country." Al Gore had lost his beloved mother, and the nation had lost a heroic and distinguished lady who had made a big impact upon

---

123 Adam Nagourney, *New York Times*, December 15, 2002..

society. Donna Brazile, Al Gore's campaign manager in 2000, stated that "She was an optimist and one of the smartest women I've ever met in politics."[124] It was a very sad time for Al and his family, and like most other families, life without his mom would never truly be the same again.

Gore would later enter into a new adventure, this time as an entrepreneur. In August 2005, he and Joel Hyatt founded the cable channel and satellite network called Current TV, headquartered in San Francisco, California. Hyatt, a prominent attorney and business-man, and former Democratic Party official, was Gore's cofounder and business partner. The concept for developing Current TV was to provide a different approach to news and events than the traditional cable and television Networks. It also targeted young, educated citi-zens by providing viewer-created content and citizen journalism. It would also be dedicated to the coverage of events and issues that the traditional networks were not giving a voice to. The network would cover issues such as the environment, famine, poverty, civil liber-ties, and some controversial issues that the other networks refused to show. Gore stated that the cable channel would be non-political and would focus on the issues. As he noted in an interview with Amazon: "What we are trying to do in part, is to provide a public forum for viewers to submit content about issues of concern to them. And they have, by the thousands, on issues from the War in Iraq to the environment to education and others". "I am continually amazed by both the quality of the submission and the breadth and depth of the subject matter",[125]Gore said. The network successfully launched in 2005 and began to show progress. However, by 2010, program ratings had declined, and in 2011 the network made both personnel and programming changes. Several television executives and com-mentators from other networks were hired, including Elliott Spitzer and Joy Bahar, and the network seems to be enjoying a new wave of interest and viewership.

---

124 Boston.com. December 16, 2004.
125 Al Gore, Amazon interview, 2007.

CHAPTER 14

The Oscar and the Nobel

As I'm writing this paragraph, sitting here in my office, the temperature outside is 109 degrees, on this late June day in 2012. Some places across the state of Tennessee and most parts of the Midwest and Southeast have reported temperatures as high as 114 degrees, breaking the all-time records for recorded temperatures. And while I did not write this book to debate the merits of global warming or the climate crisis—I will leave that to others to debate—I can't help but wonder, in the back of my mind, if just maybe everything that Al Gore has talked about in his books seems to be happening, however prophetic it may seem. So it is with that open mind that I myself, like many others, feel the need to at least explore the possibility that what vice president Gore believes to be true, may be actually happening, whether it is an inconvenient truth or not.

Al Gore would write another book, which was a follow-up to *Earth in the Balance*. The book, *An Inconvenient Truth*, would be another best seller for Gore. It was published in 2006, and within weeks it would land on the *New York Times* best seller list. Sales of the book soared, as did Gore's popularity. Gore made a book tour across the country promoting the book, as long lines of fans and supporters waited to meet the former vice president and have their books autographed. Gore could not be happier with the response, and his life had now taken on a new dimension.

In the book, Gore delves deeply into the science of the global warming and climate crises and frames the issues in such a way that allows an easy understanding of a rather complex subject. He outlines a set of truths about the planet, one being that the "atmosphere is thin enough that we are capable of changing its composition," and another being that "almost all of the mountain glaciers in the world are now melting, many of them quite rapidly." He says the cause of these environmental changes can be traced to the "correlation between temperatures and CO2 concentrations over the last 1,000 years."[126] By reviewing the records over time, scientists can tell from the ice cores what the amount of temperature has risen over time. Gore explains that the greenhouse gases (carbon dioxide, methane, nitrous oxide, etc.) within the earth's atmosphere are causing the earth's ozone layer to become depleted. This leads to an increased exposure to the sun's rays, resulting in an increase in the climate's temperature. In return, the rising temperatures have created extreme weather conditions, affecting the entire planet. Gore also states that temperatures are increasing all over the world, including the oceans'. This increase in temperatures has been more dramatic the last forty to fifty years, resulting in more flooding, hurricanes, tornados, typhoons, cyclones, and drought.[127]

The vice president says that some of the causes of the increase in CO2 levels are pollution, primarily chemicals and hazardous waste that have been dumped into our rivers and streams. Also the release of CO2 and other chemicals from automobiles, factories, refrigerators, and other human activities have contributed to the problem. Gore believes that the climate crisis is primarily human made, and it is humans that will ultimately either continue to contribute to the

---

126 Al Gore, *An Inconvenient Truth* (2006).
127 Ibid.

problem or finally solve the crisis.[128] Gore suggests that mankind must act rapidly and with urgency if we are to solve the climate crisis, and says, "The truth about the climate crisis is an inconvenient one that means we are going to have to change the way we live our lives. Now it is up to us to use our democracy and our God-given ability to reason with one another about our future and make moral choices to change the policies and behaviors that would, if continued, leave a degraded, diminished, and hostile planet for our children and grandchildren and for humankind." In wrapping up the book, Al Gore makes a powerful statement on the future of the climate crisis, telling his readers that "We must choose instead to make the 21st century a time of renewal. By seizing the opportunity that is bound up in this crisis, we can unleash the creativity, innovation, and inspiration that are just as much a part of our human birthright as our vulnerability to greed and pettiness. The choice is ours. The responsibility is ours. The future is ours. "The truth about the climate crisis is an inconvenient one that means we are going to have to change the way we live our lives."[129]

After the book's success, Gore was approached by David Guggenheim, a Hollywood director, about the possibility of turning the book into a documentary film. Initially Gore was reluctant, fearing that it would be difficult to pull off. But he finally relented, and in 2006, the production and filming of the documentary began. Lawrence Bender, of *Pulp Fiction* fame, and Laurie David, wife of Seinfeld co-creator Larry David, were the producers. The premise of *An Inconvenient Truth*, the film, was to show Gore behind the scenes, during his traveling "power point slide show" on the climate crisis, traveling across the world giving the same presentation to audience after audience. He would deliver the same slide presentation to small groups of environmental activists numbering one hundred to two hundred people, and often to large convention audiences of four thousand to five thousand people.

His road show was like that of a gospel preacher, spreading the word to anyone who would listen. He would fill his schedule with

---

128 Ibid.
129 Ibid.

stops in cities like New York, Chicago, Los Angeles, and in smaller towns like Long Beach, California, and Eugene, Oregon. All along the way he took the same slides and presented the same speech, warning the people of the imminent threat of global warming. Gore begins the documentary with a very powerful commentary: "You look at that river gently flowing by. You notice the leaves rustling with the wind. You hear the birds you hear the tree frogs. In the distance you hear a cow. You feel the grass. The mud gives a little bit on the river bank. It's quite…it's peaceful. And all of a sudden it's a gear shift inside you. And it's like taking a deep breath and going. Oh yeah I forgot about this." Gore states that "Global Warming causes not only more flooding, but also more draught. One of the reasons for this has to do with the fact that Global Warming not only increases precipitation worldwide, but also relocates the precipitation."[130]

He also reveals that the presidential election caused him to refocus on the issue: "It brought (Presidential Election) into clear focus the mission that I had been pursuing for all these years, and I started giving the slide show again."[131] The proceeds from the sale of the book and documentary were donated to the Alliance for Climate Change. This further demonstrated that Al Gore was not only talking the talk, he was also literally putting his money where his mouth was. The film was a huge success, generating more than $49 million at the box office, ranking it the nation's third highest grossing documentary film in history. It also sold more than 1.5 million DVDs worldwide, and has been rated as one of the all-time greatest documentaries.[132]

In June 2006, Al Gore founded the nonprofit organization called The Climate Project (TCP). Based out of Nashville, Tennessee, TCP was formed to create ideas and educate the public on the climate crisis. It was also designed to help increase awareness of the climate crisis through communication and training. Gore also believed that the TCP would help propel the federal and state governments to enact legislation that would help to solve the climate crisis. TCP

---

130 Ibid.

131 Ibid.

132 Steve Gorman, *Los Angeles Times*, February 26, 2007.

included a website with daily news articles and announcements about the environment and the climate crisis. It also was a clearinghouse for communication and training on the climate crisis. Gore personally conducted training presentations to thousands of people. TCP later merged with another environmental group and became known as "The Climate Reality Project."

It was now 2007, and it would prove to be one of Al Gore's best years ever. The year began with Gore's documentary film *An Inconvenient Truth* winning an Oscar for best documentary feature. Oscars were also awarded to director Davis Guggenheim and producers Lawrence Bender and Laurie David. Gore accepted the award on stage at the Academy Awards. Gore took the opportunity to tell the world about the threat of global warming. He stated, "My fellow Americans, people all over the world, we need to solve the climate crisis. It's not a political issue, it's a moral issue. We have everything we need to get started with the possible exception of the will to act. That's a renewable resource. Let's renew it." Gore received a standing ovation from the audience, and backstage many movie stars greeted him like a king. He took pictures with them and talked with them. But it was Al Gore who was the star of the night. The big night for Gore would further his popularity throughout the nation and world. And in many Democratic Party circles, his name was at the top of their list for presidential candidates. There were a number of Democratic Party activists and fundraisers that were urging Gore to run for President in 2007. In Gore they saw someone that was passionate and dedicated to their causes. Someone who was an experienced leader that brought an enormous amount of talent. Gore could also count on a devoted following in political and cultural circles, and would be able to raise unlimited amounts of money. Even Steve Jobs went on record urging Gore to make another run. He stated that "we have dug ourselves into a 20 ft. hole and we need somebody who knows how to build a ladder. Al's the guy," said Jobs. "Like many others I have tried my best to convince him. So far no luck."[133]

---

133 Eric Pooley, *Time*, May 16, 2007.

Oslo, Norway, is one of the most beautiful cities in the world. Located at the southern end of Norway, in Northern Europe, Oslo is situated between a large peninsula to its south, surrounded by green hills and mountains to its north. It is an almost perfect setting geographically, and close to perfection both culturally and politically. It was in this culturally and economically important port city that a man from Carthage, Tennessee, would be honored with one of his greatest awards yet. Some sixty years earlier, a man from the same Carthage, Cordell Hull, the former United States Secretary of State, from 1933 to 1944, had been awarded the Nobel Prize for his efforts in establishing the United Nations, in an effort to make peace throughout the world.

It was October 2007, and Vice President Gore was busy as always, simultaneously juggling three or four projects, just the normal stuff for the multitasking, multitalented vice president. Only on this day he would find time to enjoy a pleasant surprise. He received a phone call and was told that he had been awarded the Nobel Peace Prize for his work and commitment to the environment, sharing the award with the United Nations Intergovernmental Panel on Climate Change. Gore and the UN panel were awarded the Nobel Peace Prize for their work and efforts "to build up and disseminate greater knowledge about man-made climate change, and to lay the foundations for the measures that are needed to counteract such change."[134] World leaders, from presidents to kings and queens, congratulated Gore on receiving the award. Gore spoke at the awards ceremony in Oslo, Norway, on December 10, 2007. He took to the stage and said that he was "deeply honored" to accept the award. His speech was entitled "Our Purpose." In the speech, he outlined the urgency that the human race faces in dealing with the climate crisis, comparing the situation to what mankind faced in fighting and winning the battles against war and diseases and struggling for civil rights. He stated that the climate crisis is "the greatest challenge we've ever faced." "We face a true planetary emergency. The climate crisis is not a political issue, it is a moral and spiritual challenge to all of humanity," said Gore. He also mentioned Cordell Hull, the other man

---

134 The Nobel Foundation, 2007.

from Carthage, and compared his efforts in trying to bring peace to the world to the climate crisis and the responsibility that our generation is now faced with. As he ended the speech, he said the climate crisis affects "our ability to live on Planet Earth – to have a future as a civilization," adding that he believes "this is a moral issue. "It is our time to rise again to secure our future". The audience was captivated and gave Gore an overwhelming ovation. He had finally been recognized by the world for his efforts, and this was undoubtedly one of Gore's finest hours. Gore's popularity had now risen to an all-time high, with his worldwide appeal surpassing that of even presidents. It was another remarkable achievement for the man who had spent most of his life trying to help fix the climate crisis. Later in the same year, *Time* magazine named Gore the runner-up its Man of the Year award. In honor of his great year of service to the world, Bono wrote an article on Al Gore for *Time*. In the article, Bono stated that "Al Gore is the kind of leader these times require. Not as President— God and the Electoral College have given him a different job." "As it happens, Al is at work repositioning his country from the inside out as a leader in clean energy; and along the way restoring faith in the U.S. as a moral powerhouse that can lead a great, global spiritual revival as the temperature rises." It was one of the most admiring and passionate articles that anyone has ever written about Gore. Bono had summed up for everyone just what Al Gore meant to the world.[135] It was truly a remarkable year for Gore. Indeed the year 2007 seemed to be the time that Al Gore had finally won the race of his life. His efforts on the environment and climate change had now been fully recognized, but it would not be the end of his efforts. He would view it as another opportunity to further advance his cause, now that the world had given him attention.

---

135 Bono, *Time*, December 19, 2007.

CHAPTER 15

A New Crusade

"I am Al Gore, and I used to be the next President of the United States", the man in the navy blue suit said as the audience erupted in laughter. It was vintage Al Gore who was still showing a good sense of humor, making fun of his misfortune, while appearing to be having the time of his life. And throughout most of the decade since the Supreme Court had sealed his political fate, Al Gore had stayed out of politics, very rarely criticizing President Bush and the political establishment. But all that changed in 2007, when Gore released another new book, entitled *The Assault on Reason*, a book about the political and social state of America. It was Al Gore's return to politics, and presented his take on the state of our government and society. Eric Pooley of *Time* magazine wrote: "The book is a patient, meticulous examination of how the participatory democracy envisioned by our founders has gone awry, how the American marketplace of ideas has gradually devolved into a home-shopping network of 30-second ads and mall-tested phrases."[136] The book is well written but also very deep in its analysis of democracy and society. It also allows the reader a glimpse into what kind of President Al Gore would have been and the issues that he is most concerned about. In the book, Gore outlines his views on our democracy. He states that our Founding Fathers relied upon a "well-informed" citizenry to reason in its decisions and actions. Gore believes that fear is the single greatest threat to our democracy, and if our political leaders rule on the basis of fear, then our freedom and democracy becomes flawed. He believes that our government today has become a hostage to fear, and our politicians have used the war on terror as a tool to expound our citizen's fears, resulting in a decline in our freedoms. He specifically calls out President George Bush and his administration, stating that they "misused fear to manipulate the political process." In the process, our free speech and civil liberties have been suppressed. Gore states that "history will surely judge America's decision to invade and occupy" Iraq as a "decision that was not only tragic but absurd." He also deliberates on the politics of wealth, and says that they are the greatest threat to democracy. But Gore not only outlines the problems that are confronting our nation, he also delivers answers to help solve the problems and "restore the rule of reason."[137]

Al Gore continued to turn up the heat on the climate crisis anywhere he could find an ear. He testified before Congress, warning them of the dangers of global warming and the effects it would have on the nation if we didn't address the problem. And he urged them to pass legislation that would help to solve the problem. He said the issue of global warming should be "non-political" and something that all Americans would eventually concede to if only its politicians, business leaders, and communities would be told the truth, and if only people would use sound reason after looking at the facts. To that end, on July 7, 2007, Gore presided over the Live Earth concert event, the worldwide televised rock concert that was staged to bring

---

136 Eric Pooley, *Time*, May 16, 2007.
137 Al Gore, *The Assault on Reason* (2007).

awareness to the climate crisis. The concert was a major success, with well over one billion participants across seven continents.

The work that Gore was doing appeared to be paying off. A *New York Times*/CBS poll conducted in 2007 showed that a majority of Democrats (90 percent), Republicans (60 percent), and Independents (80 percent) favored action to address the climate crisis. But even though public opinion polls clearly show that a majority of Americans believe the crisis is a real threat to the world, the right-wing conservative elements of society continue to deny that there is an issue. At every opportunity, they take on Gore and try to undermine his claims, even though in most cases the scientific community agrees with what Gore has said. Those who disagree with Gore seem to be more concerned with making the climate crisis a political issue, rather than using reason and reality in acknowledging the many scientific truths. But Al Gore is determined to continue the fight, and with each stone that a critic throws, Gore seems to become more resolute in his crusade.

As we enter a new decade in the twenty-first century, Al Gore continues to evolve into one of the more powerful and influential people in the world. He has gone from vice president to environmental crusader, to entrepreneur, often wearing several hats at once. In so doing his image has changed, and with it his influence and power. Today Al Gore leads and chairs the Climate Reality Project, which he founded in June 2006. The Climate Reality Project has more than five million members and supporters across the world. The project's goal is to inform and educate people around the world on the climate crisis, and to explain that "it is real and we know how to solve it." As the chairman of Climate Reality, Gore is at the helm of a project that is having a major impact on the climate crisis.[138]

Gore also is an advocate and investor in green energy, serving as chairman of Generation Investment Management, a company that focuses on investing in green energy technology and environmental friendly companies. In November 2009, Gore's venture capital firm in Silicon Valley (Kleiner Perkins Caufield & Byers) agreed to invest in a company called Silver Spring Networks. The company

---

138 The Climate Reality Project, 2011.

develops hardware and software for electricity grids, in an effort to make the delivery of electricity more efficient. Al has also put some of his private investments into green energy technology. In investing in green energy, Gore has been able to deflect criticism from some of the critics of climate change. In an interview with Diane Sawyer on *Good Morning America*, he stated, "I am proud to put my money where my mouth is for the past 30 years," "And though that is not the majority of my business activities, I absolutely believe in investing in accordance with my beliefs and my values."[139]

In 2009, Al Gore wrote yet another book on the environment, entitled Our *Choice*, which is a follow-up to *An Inconvenient Truth*. It is Gore's effort to provide solutions for the climate crisis. In the introduction, Gore outlines the key premise of the book: "It is abundantly clear that we have at our fingertips all of the tools we need to solve the climate crisis. The only missing ingredient is collective will". "We can solve the crisis. It will be hard, to be sure, but if we can make the choice to solve it, I have no doubt whatsoever that we can and will succeed."[140] Gore outlines his beliefs that our society must take action to use alternative energy at every opportunity presented. He specifically points out the need to generate more electricity via the sun and wind: "Electricity can be produced from sunlight in two main ways—by producing heat that powers an electricity generator or by converting sunlight directly to electricity using solar cells." He says that the wind is actually another form of the sun's energy, and he advocates the use of more energy from wind sources. Gore also recommends using geothermal energy, or natural hot spots on earth, as another means of using alternative energy sources. Geothermal systems that allow home heating and cooling can be put into place. He also talks about the need to grow more alternative fuels, such as ethanol, miscanthus grass, and organic materials, which will dramatically reduce the amounts of oil and CO_2 based energy sources that the world consumes. Then Gore turns to solutions in capturing carbon dioxide that is presently being emitted into the atmosphere. He states that "the idea of 'carbon capture and sequestration'

---

139 ABC News, November 3, 2009.
140 Al Gore, *Our Choice* (2009), Introduction.

(CCS) is compelling" and "in theory the world could capture all of the CO2 that is presently emitted into the atmosphere by fossil fuel electricity plants and sequester it safely in repositories located deep underground and beneath the bottom of the ocean." Gore also talks about how society can change the way we use energy, and that "less is more." He talks about improving the "Super Grids" to make them more efficient. With these changes, we could dramatically reduce current energy consumption.

At the end of the book, Gore offers an analysis of the obstacles that are preventing more action on the climate crisis, saying that "changing the way we think" about energy usage is vitally important. He also says that it is the "political obstacles" that are the greatest roadblocks for changing the way the world reacts in trying to solve the climate crisis. He ends the book with another powerful point of persuasion: "The choice is awesome and potentially eternal. It is in the hands of the present generation: a decision we cannot escape, and a choice to be mourned or celebrated through all the generations that follow."[141]

Gore continues to try to convince the political establishment to take more aggressive measures in the fight against the climate crisis. And while President Obama and the Democratic-controlled Congress made many major strides in 2009 (i.e., enacting fuel efficiency standards for automobiles, pushing the EPA to enforce the Clean Air Act, and making hundreds of changes in environmental and energy policy), he has failed in many ways. Gore stated that "in spite of these and other achievements, President Obama has thus far failed to use the bully pulpit to make the case for bold action on climate change. After successfully passing his green stimulus package, he did nothing to defend it when Congress decimated its funding. After the House passed cap and trade, he did little to make passage in the Senate a priority." Gore said, "without presidential leadership that focuses intensely on making the public aware of the reality we face, nothing will change."[142]

---

141 Al Gore. *Our Choice.* 2009.
142 Al Gore, *Rolling Stone,* June 22, 2011.

While Gore has been disappointed with President Obama on the environment, he is still optimistic about the grassroots support of people across the world. "All over the world, the grassroots movement in favor of changing public policies to confront the climate crisis and build a more prosperous, sustainable future is growing rapidly," Gore said. But he reiterates that unless governments take more action, it will prolong the crisis and take more time before the movement can truly begin to make progress in solving the climate crisis.[143]

In 2011, Apple Founder and Chairman Steve Jobs passed away after a long battle with cancer. Jobs and Gore were close personal friends, and had developed a very good working relationship with each other the last few years. Gore was one of the speakers at Jobs eulogy, and he gave a very eloquent and touching tribute to the man, at one point saying that Jobs was a man that who 'only comes around every 250 years'.

In an interview with Walt Mossberg of *All Things D*, Gore shared his thoughts on the impact that Steve Jobs had on the world. "Steves greatest accomplishment was Apple itself. "He created an organization –and inspired it—that literally creates technology that people love…and that's going to continue", Gore said. "There are so many things down the pipeline, and the team that he built is hitting on all cylinders". Gore also said that Jobs molded a strong team and they had discussions at their board meetings about cultivating a strong and robust team. "No one will ever replace him (Jobs), and yet he served on the Board at Disney, and he used to talk about after Walt Disney died, the company always got into trouble about asking what would Walt do in this situation. And he made it very clear that I don't want that" (at Apple), Gore said. [144]

Gore continues to exercise tremendous influence on the Apple Board, and is looked upon with great respect by the company and its leaders. He not only provides the company with leadership and keen knowledge of understanding the complexities of computer technology, he also provides Apple with incite into the worlds economic and

---

143 Ibid.

144 Walt Mossberg and Peter Kafka, *All Things D*, , October 20, 2011

political issues. And of course he offers his advice on environmental issues where the company has shown enormous leadership and commitment to the environment. Al is also in much demand as a speaker and talk show guest, and travels the world continuing to play a role in the climate change crisis.

Al Gore has been successful at almost everything he has ever tried to do. Indeed the pace and intensity that he puts into each project and adventure leaves the observer wondering how this man inherited all of his enormous abilities. The last time I spoke with him, he expressed his disappointment in not being elected president. But I sensed that he was now very comfortable just being private citizen Al Gore. In private he will tell you that he believes there were more people in Florida who voted for him than George Bush, and he also believes the Supreme Court was politically motivated in their ruling to stop the recounts. But he has been very gracious in the way he has handled the situation, and has moved on with his life, finding peace in a life outside of politics.

He genuinely enjoys being at the forefront of the climate crisis and leading the Alliance for Climate Change, his work with Current TV, and serving on the board at Apple, and his other business adventures. Al also is much more relaxed than before, and does not feel the need to measure every word or sentence that he speaks. Moreover, he does not seem to be overly concerned with what the media or his critics think about him. Gore's schedule is almost as hectic as when he was Vice President. On a typical day he will spend 10 to 12 hours delving into his business responsibilities and environmental activities, always connected to his associates and partners whether he is on-line or in person. He maintains a luxury condo/apartment at the St. Regis in San Francisco, along with his home in Nashville, travelling between the two locations every other week.

I last saw Al Gore at his home in Nashville, where he invited me up for a visit so we could talk and see each other in private. After being escorted inside the house by an aide, I entered the living room where he was placing wood into the fireplace. Al suddenly turned around and greeted me with a "Hello Troy." He was very gracious and polite, and after shaking my hand he said, "Have a seat." He sat down on his sofa across the room and I took a chair next to the fireplace. He was dressed causally, wearing a pullover winter shirt, jeans, and hiking shoes. There we sat in his living room, just the two of us. We talked about our families and life in general, and even managed to talk a little about politics and government, sharing our thoughts on the current dysfunctional political process, both agreeing that the process is broken. I congratulated him on his many accomplishments since he left public service, including serving on the board at Apple and his work with Current TV. We also talked about life and how short it really can be, recalling friends that we had lost. As we were talking I mentioned to him that I was distressed over the recent losses in my life. He recommended that I read a couple of books, including *The Road Less Traveled*, by Scott Peck. He recited the first paragraph of the book from memory and also suggested that I pray and meditate during the day. As I sat in the chair across the room from him, I thought to myself how special and unique the man really is, and how blessed I've been to have him as a friend. This moment had summed up for me the essence of Al Gore the man. He is someone who is complicated and gifted, caring and loyal, with an insatiable desire to make a positive difference on the country-and the world. He has been misunderstood by many, but admired by the vast majority. He continues to inspire and surprise, and will be remembered as one of the most influential and fascinating public figures in history.

What would Al Gore have done as President?

In looking back on history and the political career of Al Gore, one has to wonder what kind of President Al Gore would have been. How would he have governed, and how differently than George W. Bush? In reviewing all of Gore's comments in interviews and speeches after the election, there are many conclusions that are credible and valid.

To begin with, in his first term as president, one could expect that his administration would have tried to govern from a point of strength, with clarity and purpose. He most assuredly would have tried to address the issues that he addressed in his campaign, such as education, economic expansion, health care, environment and civil liberties. It is also safe to presume that Gore would have continued most of the Clinton legacy, focusing upon the expansion of free trade and high technology initiatives; stimulating the economy and providing help to the middle and lower class; while providing accountability and oversight for government programs and services. There is one event, however, that would have required Al Gore to steer off course somewhat. The terrorist attacks on the United States would have caused Gore to alter some of his decisions as president. He most certainly would have made the decision to invade Afghanistan. There is little evidence to suggest otherwise. I believe Gore would have acted swiftly and decisively in dismantling the Al Qaeda operations that were based in Afghanistan. The vice president, in 2002, stated that the "war on terror" and the terrorists located in Afghanistan would have been his main priorities. But what Gore clearly would have done differently than President Bush is in how he responded to Iraq. Al Gore would not have made the decision to invade Iraq. He has repeatedly stated this, and in his book *The Assault on Reason*, he makes a clear and compelling case in how the Bush administration made a drastic mistake by invading Iraq. A President Gore also would not have allowed the war on terror to be used as a tool to infringe upon the nations basic freedoms (e.g., spying on Americans without due process, torture of prisoners at Guantanamo Bay, a police-state presence at airports, etc.). Gore would later say that he "would have patiently organized an international coalition (against Iraq). I think we should put the war against terror as our No. 1 priority, and not lose focus on that."

He specifically calls out President George W. Bush and his administration, stating that they "misused fear to manipulate the political process." In the process, our free speech and civil liberties have been suppressed. Gore states that "history will surely judge America's decision to invade and occupy" Iraq as a "decision that was not only tragic but absurd." In a 2002 interview on CNN's *Larry King Live*, Gore provided his clear opinion on how the war on terror should be conducted. "Well the fear—the fear is warranted, but the remedy needs to be matched to the threat. The objective of the terrorists is to destroy our way of life. "We should not give them part of their victory by destroying important parts of our own way of life." "And a right to privacy is a part of every American's right. No we want nothing like that (Big Brother type state) in the United States. We will cast our lot with free speech and openness and the rights of the individual."

Al Gore would also have respected the "rule of law, the rights of our individual citizens, and the need to abide by the international laws and treaties". He stated in his book the Assault on Reason, that President Bush and his administration had created a White House in which anyone who disagreed with its policies were treated with contempt and assault, and in some cases even fired or discredited because of their beliefs. Indeed, Vice President Gore made it clear in his remarks and commentary that suggest a Gore Administration would have not tolerated any sort of misconduct, and instead his White House would have been one open to other ideas and viewpoints, encouraging different thoughts and reasoning in regards to issues and policy. In the Foreign Policy arena, it is safe to say that Gore would have used more diplomacy in his dealings with the rest of the world. He would have maintained the United States 'Sovereignty', while also abiding by International Laws and Treaties, demonstrating a sincere desire to cooperate fully with the U.S. allies, while also extending opportunities for peace with our enemies. I also believe that Al Gore would have tried to broker a peace deal with Israel and the Palestinians, continuing the Clinton policy that was somewhat successful in the 1990's. Gore clearly believes that Israel is a strong friend and ally of the United States, and he has demonstrated his personal thoughts in his past record in Congress and also as Vice President. But he also recognizes that Peace in the Middle East must also involve recognizing the Palestinians, and treating them with respect, knowing that the U.S. has strong relationships with many Arab Nations who have legitimately demonstrated their desire for stability and peace.

Moreover, Al Gore would have focused much more on domestic issues, such as the economy, education, healthcare, environment, campaign finance reform, veterans affairs, etc. Gore would have been much more engaged and active on the economy, continuing to stimulate and regulate the enormous growth and prosperity that he had helped to oversee during the Clinton-Gore administration. He would have also been much more engaged and active on the economy. He would have focused on creating millions of new high –tech and green energy jobs through his leadership in technology and the environment, thus bolstering what was already a robust economy heading into the new century.

Gore would have focused on America's infrastructure in building new roads and structures. And without the billions of dollars spent on the War in Iraq, Al Gore would have been able to provide more resources to job creation and the economy. He also would have addressed the inequalities of income and tried to improve the gap between the lower and upper income levels. Al Gore also would not have provided tax cuts for the wealthy as President Bush did when he took office, and as a result trillions of dollars of revenue would have been saved. In the process it is likely that the United States would not have experienced the great recession that crippled the economy at the end of 2008 and into 2012. At a minimum it is safe to assert that any recession would not have been as severe without the two wars being fought simultaneously. But what Gore would have done differently is that he would have ensured that the big banks and Wall Street were regulated more effectively. During the Bush Administration, the nation saw an unprecedented amount of cut-backs in regulation and oversight. Al Gore would have recognized as he did as while he was in Congress that the large corporations and industries cannot be trusted to regulate themselves entirely. But he also would not have been anti-business as many people may believe. One only has to look at his role in the Clinton administration, and his leadership on Commerce issues, that he would have allowed for "free enterprise". Gore also would have continued the expansion of the Computer Information Age, while ensuring that all citizens across the world have "open and free access" to information and sharing of content. But he would have also been concerned about the potential abuse of the "internet providers" and their attempts at limiting the content and sharing of information. Gore states that the providers "have an economic incentive to extend their control over the physical infrastructure of the network to leverage control of Internet content." If they went about it the wrong way, they could potentially violate the Federal Communication Act. Gore also stated that "in the 1990's the Clinton-Gore administration made conscious choice to impose few regulations" on the industry in order to preserve the unique relationship that the internet medium provides.

Gore would have been a friend to small businesses as he had demonstrated when he was in Congress. He would have fought for tax relief for small businesses and provided funding for business incentives and investments, making it easier for businesses to operate and stay profitable. In the same arena, he would have fought hard for tax relief on the middle and lower classes while ensuring that the top one percent of Americans pay their fair share.

Al Gore also would have become the first real environmental President in leading the United States as a leader on the world stage on environmental policies, and finally confronting the climate crisis by putting it at the forefront of US environmental policy. A Gore administration would have initiated measures aimed at preventing further global warming and climate change. He would have supported the Environmental Protection Agency (EPA) in its efforts in protecting the environment, and further enhancing and strengthening laws and regulations. Gore would have proposed sweeping measures on the environment aimed at protecting our natural resources and habitat, while preserving millions of acres of wetlands, public lands and endangered species. Under a President Gore, the nation would have ushered in green energy alternatives to oil and provided incentives to businesses and state governments. As a result the environment would have been given more attention, and Al Gore would have been the best friend to the National Parks since Teddy Roosevelt

Moreover, Gore would have been very concerned with education and would have increased spending in the areas of technology, training and other educational advancements. He would have viewed the Federal Government as a key to bringing forth a well educated society that could better compete with the rest of the world.

And while a President Gore would have exercised more foreign policy diplomacy, he also would have been a strong advocate of national defense, as he demonstrated when he was a United States senator. He would have ensured that the American troops were well equipped with the latest and best technology and weapons, pressuring the Pentagon to implement more advanced weapons systems, while eliminating waste and shutting down defense contracts that were outdated and not vital to national security. He would have been particularly interested in new technology that advanced our defense capabilities but also saved taxpayer money in the process. NASA and the Space programs would have been well funded, and space exploration would have continued beyond his presidency. Looking back there is also one event that stands out where President Gore would have governed differently than George Bush. The hurricane Katrina disaster would have been dealt with much more differently. Al would have ensured that the Federal Government responded with promptness and forcefulness in the days before Katrina hit New Orleans, thereby saving lives and lessening the severity of the devastation. It is also safe to reason that the Federal Emergency Management Agency would have been given more resources and greater leadership. The Supreme Court would have also looked differently than the current makeup that includes five conservative justices. Al Gore would have been able to appoint the replacement for Chief Justice Rehnquist, and he most assuredly would have selected a more moderate judge as Rehnquist's successor. In addition, Al Gore would have appointed hundreds of federal judges across the nation, with most of his appointments being judges with moderate philosophies. In his dealing with Congress, Gore would also have governed differently. I believe that he would have demonstrated moderation in his dealings with the US Congress. It is clear that he is concerned with the current dysfunction in the Congress, but also with the increased power of the Executive branch of Government. Thus it is reasonable to suggest that Gore would have used his experience and skills in compromising with both the democrats and republicans in trying to build consensus on issues that should not be political in nature. He would have tried to move beyond the partisan politics that have divided and crippled our government the last twenty years. Gore would also not have undermined the legislative branch in exercising more executive control as was seen during the Bush administration. There is no question that Al Gore would have stood up for his principles and political philosophy, but he would have been more willing to compromise for the good of the people than President Bush demonstrated in his dealings with Congress In short, Al Gore would have been known as a domestic president instead of a wartime president. The United States would have been governed very differently, and the entire world would be a different place today.

In the end, one has to ponder that a Gore presidency was not meant to be. There are far too many events and sequences in which the election should have been won by Gore, but the odds were not in his favor. Yet there is no question that the majority of voters in Florida, and the nation, went to the polls on November 5th 2000 with their intent to elect Al Gore as President of the United States. Whatever the circumstances and fate, the end result is that the man who was inaugurated on that cold January day in 2001 should have been Al Gore. In this case, the peoples will did not prevail in our democracy, leaving history to judge this event critically and harshly.

Al Gore Achievements and Personal Information

Born: March 31, 1948, Washington, D.C.
Home: Nashville, Tennessee
Married: Mary Elizabeth "Tipper" Aitcheson
Children: Karen, born August 6, 1973
            Kristin, born June 5, 1977
            Sarah, born January 7, 1979
            Albert III, born October 19, 1982

Career:

Vice President of the United States: 1993-2001
United State Senator, 1985-1993
United States Congressman, 1977-1985
Nobel Laureate, 2007
Chairman and Co-Founder, Current TV

Chairman and Co-Founder, Generation Investment Management
Board Member, Apple Inc.
Senior Advisor, Google Inc.
Partner, Kleiner Perkins Caufield & Byers
Visiting Professor, Middle Tennessee State University,
Columbia University School of Journalism, Fisk University,
and the University of California, Los Angeles (UCLA).

Awards:

Nobel Peace Prize Award, 2007
Grammy Award, for Best Spoken Word Album for *An Inconvient Truth*, 2009
Emmy Award, for *Current TV*, 2007
Webby Award, 2005
Time Magazine, 2007 Person of Year, runner-up
National Father of the Year, 1984

Vice Presidential Achievements:

National Performance Review of 1993 – led the review of the US Government and authored report which was submitted to President Clinton. The majority of the recommendations were enacted into law by President Clinton and Congress.

NAFTA – authored much of the language in the bill and broke the tie in the US Senate. Signed into law by President Bill Clinton.

Telecommunications Act of 1996 – authored much of the language in the bill. Signed into law by President Bill Clinton.

Small Business Tax Relief Bill – cast the tie breaking vote as Vice President in the US Senate that provided 90% of small businesses with tax relief in 1993 as part of economic package which increased the expensing limit and provided targeted capital gains tax cuts for more than 90% of small businesses.

Information Technology Agreement - Vice President Gore worked to increase High Technology Trade with Asian Pacific Nations. At the 1996 APEC Summit, the Clinton-Gore administration reached a tariff agreement known as the Information Technology Agreement. This agreement affects the worldwide technology trade market, and has helped to create jobs and expand technology throughout Asia and the world.

Promoted the growth of Electronic Commerce. In July 1997, President Bill Clinton and Vice President Al Gore announced strategy for promoting electronic commerce by establishing a global framework for promoting and outlining an agenda for international discussions and agreements to facilitate the growth of electronic commerce.

Legislative Achievements (US House and Senate):

Author, Information Infrastructure and Technology Act of 1992 – designed to speed the introduction of technologies into schools, hospitals, businesses, etc.

Author and principle sponsor, High Performance Computing and Communications Act of 1991, signed into law by President George H.W. Bush. Established computing technology and information superhighway (internet).

Sponsor, Working Families Tax Relief Act of 1991 - the act provided relief to 135 million middle and lower income Americans by cutting taxes for some families by more than $ 900 million.

Co-sponsor of Enterprise Formation Act of 1991 - bill designed to allow for small business tax deductions.

Sponsor, Supercomputer Network Act of 1986 - bill provided funds to develop and study communication methods for universities and Federal Research Facilities to develop future network options.

Author and principle sponsor, National Organ Donor Network Act of 1984, signed into law by President Reagan.

Author and sponsor, Small Business Innovation Act of 1982, signed into law by President Reagan.

Principle sponsor, Infant Formula Act of 1980, signed into law by President Carter.

Co-author and principle sponsor, Superfund Act of 1980 (Comprehensive Environmental Response, Compensation and Liability Act). Signed into law by President Carter.

Author and principle sponsor, Sodium content legislation.

Strategic arms control, author, principle sponsor, a plan to reduce nuclear arms and eliminate the fear of a first strike by global super-powers (this plan gained wide support from members of Congress from both parties and was adopted by the Reagan administration as the position in strategic arms negotiations with the Soviet Union.

Genetic engineering legislation, author, principle sponsor, to establish a presidential commission to monitor the science of human genetic engineering, conducted landmark hearings on the implications of human, animal, and plant gene manipulation.

Strategic Petroleum Reserve, led congressional effort to establish a reserve of energy resources for emergency purposes.

Computer education software legislation, author, principle sponsor, would establish public/private corporation to help improve the quality of computer education software, conducted landmark hearings on the issue.

Veteran's disability compensation, principle sponsor, author of legislation to grant compensation to veterans suffering from wartime exposure to atomic tests.

Cigarette warming labels, author, principle sponsor, a compromise legislative agreement between the tobacco industry and health care community over new warnings to the public of the dangers of smoking.

Open Meetings with Constituents – since he was in Congress, Gore held an average of four open meetings a week in every community in his congressional district. He also held more than 10 workshops in his congressional district, including workshops on tobacco issues, dairy issues, social security, solar, handicapped issues, farm disaster relief, small business issues, education, federal grants for local governments, federal health programs, preventive healthcare, etc.

Voting Attendance Record – while in Congress, Al Gore maintained an 98% voting attendance record. Congressional Quarterly Magazine.

House of Representatives

Member, House Energy and Commerce Committee
Member, Oversight and Investigations Subcommittee
Member, Telecommunications, Consumer Protection and Finance Subcommittee
Member, Energy, Conservation and Power Subcommittee
Member, House Select Committee on Intelligence Committee
Chairman, Investigations and Oversight Subcommittee
Member, Transportation, Aviation and Materials Subcommittee

Al Gore's Views on the Issues

Education – "America can compete for the future by giving our children the best schools on earth. We need to make classrooms smaller, make the school year longer and pay teachers more in return." Al Gore for President Campaign Committee, 1988.

Economy – "We can restore economic growth by getting back to basics—rebuilding our manufacturing base, straightening out our fiscal policy, and providing working Americans the training and skills they need to get ahead." Al Gore for President Campaign Committee, 1988.

Farming – "The administration's farm policies are forcing many families to give up on farming. As a farmer, I know that we must act now to preserve our family farms. We should start by doubling the conservation reserve and focusing on rural economic development." Al Gore for President Campaign Committee, 1988.

Families – "I will make sure that we have access to high-quality, affordable health care to every single child in the United States of America". Al Gore Speech in Jackson, Mississippi, February 17, 2000.

Federal Government:

"Checks and balances are vital to the functioning of our system of government. Of course it can have it's frustrations, but the founders intended that we have a system whereby no one branch has too much control over the others. Ultimately, it is up to voters to decide the control of Congress and the White House and then for elected officials to work to serve the public interest and to try to implement policies that serve the country. These are core values that are at the heart of who we are as a nation". Al Gore, Amazon interview, 2007.

Healthcare – "The need to promote affordable, quality health care services and facilities is important for Tennessee and the Nation". "In an effort to explore the state of health care in the Fourth District, I am conducting a special workshop: 'Health 79 Workshop on Health Care.'" "The program will focus on the resources available from federal and state governments and possible procedures to follow in attempts to obtain health care providers and facilities for a community. Panelists will discuss the kinds of help federal and state governments can lend and the experiences communities have had in attempting to locate health care resources." Al Gore, Congress of the United States, Jan. 5, 1979 Letter to his Tennessee 4th Congressional District Constituents.

"I am also committed to the principle of high quality, affordable health care for all. And I don't really care what kind of label people apply to those positions and view". Gore, New Hampshire Primary Debate, January 5, 2000.

Social Security – "The Social Security system will be confronted by cash flow problems in the coming year. It may also be affected by population changes expected to occur over the long-term. The purpose of the forum is to discuss these problems and to examine the options that can be chosen to make the System financially sound." By Congressman Al Gore, Congress of the United States, Letter to his Tennessee 4th Congressional District Constituents, December 6, 1982.

"I will never privatize social security or destroy it by diverting funds intended for social security. I will strengthen social security, not undermine it". Presidential Announcement, 2000.

Big Oil – "It appears that there is greater profitability in exploring for oil on the floors of the stock markets than in oil fields somewhere." There is a "hemorrhage of cash flow in an oil industry feeling secure in the green light sign" to consolidate through the "acquisitions and mergers" of smaller oil companies. Frank Gibson, *Tennessean*, December 15, 1981.

Trade – "A President must demand the removal of unfair trade barriers overseas, insisting on action rather than promises, and moving us not toward protectionism but a more open trading environment—particularly in foreign countries. We need a President who will also address factors at home that can improve our ability to compete." Al Gore for President Campaign Committee, 1988.

Israel – "I favor official American recognition of 'West Jerusalem' as Israel's Capital and moving its embassy there." Michael Widlanski, *Tennessean*, September 3, 1987.

Environment – "No goal is more crucial to healing the global environment than stabilizing human population. The rapid explosion in the number of people since the beginning of the scientific revolution and especially during the latter half of this century is the clearest single example of the dramatic change in the overall relationship between the human species and the earth's ecological system." Governments should develop an international treaty establishing limits on CO_2 emissions by country and a market for the trading of emission rights among countries that need more and countries that have an excess amount." Al Gore, *Earth in the Balance*, (1992).

Government – "Our bedrock premise is that ineffective government is not the fault of people in it. Our government is full of well-intentioned, hard-working, intelligent people—managers and staff. We intend to let our workers pursue excellence." Vice President Al Gore, Reinventing Government Summit, Philadelphia, Pennsylvania, June 25, 1993.

Government Serving People – "We are going to rationalize the way the federal government relates to the American people, and we are going to make the federal government customer friendly. A lot of people don't realize that the federal government has customers. We have customers. The American people." Vice President Al Gore,

Town Meeting, Dept. of Housing and Urban Development, March 26, 1993.

Information Age – "We are determined to move forward from an industrial age government to information age government, from a government pre-occupied with sustaining itself to a government clearly focused on serving the people." VP Al Gore, May 24, 1993, Report of the National Performance Review, September 7, 1993.

Politics as Profession – "Having been a politician for many years now, I say this from personal experience. At an early age, I learned man political skills simply by observing my parents; I also learned that these skills are valuable only insofar as they serve worthy goals. Later, I learned the visual rhetoric of my own television generation and found myself unconsciously practicing a new set of 'personality skills.' But I am increasingly struck by how easy it is for every politician—myself included—to get lost in the forms of personality traits designed to please and rhetoric designed to convey a tactical impression. Voice modulation, ten-second 'sound bites,' catchy slogans, quotable quotes, newsworthy angles, interest group buzzwords, priorities copied from pollsters reports, relaxation for effect, emotion on cue—these are the forms of modern politics, and together they can distract even the best politician from the real work at hand." Al Gore, *Earth in the Balance* (1992), 168.

Presidency:
"At least where the presidency is concerned, there is still some symmetry between the skills needed to be elected and the skills needed to govern. After all, the ability of a president to communicate effectively on television is essential. But there is this problem: while a president elected primarily because of an appealing image and personality may be able to communicate effectively, that is no guarantee that he or she can deal with the substance of government policies or provide a clear, inspiring vision of our national destiny". "Where Congress is concerned, the ability to communicate a winning personality on television is much less relevant to the skills needed after the election. A keen sense for visual rhetoric is

almost totally irrelevant to the task of writing laws—although it is, of course, quite relevant to the nearly constant work of being re-elected". Al Gore, *Earth in the Balance* (1992).

Spirituality – "It is my own belief that the image of God can be seen in every corner of creation, even in us, but only faintly. By gathering in the minds eye all of creation, one can perceive the image of the Creator vividly. "Similarly I believe that the image of the Creator, which sometimes seems so faint in the tiny corner of creation each of us beholds, is nonetheless present in its entirety—and present in us as well." Al Gore, *Earth in the Balance* (1992).

Acknowledgments

I want to recognize the people who helped me with writing this book, and without their help this book would not have been possible. First thanks to Vice President Al Gore for his help, support and friendship. He has been one of the most loyal friends I have ever had. He and his staff have given me the opportunity to tell his story and I will forever be grateful. Thanks to my niece Tiffany Martin, who read my first draft and gave me valuable advice on the final chapters. She was an inspiration to me in so many ways, but in particular in giving me the encouragement and positive feedback that enabled me to continue with the book. Thanks to my sister Rhonda Dugas for her support and encouragement to continue this book. Thanks to my friends Karen and Carter Garner for their support and friendship. Karen gave me valuable information and also allowed me to use a couple of photographs for the book. They have also been Gore friends and supporters for many years. Karen was also a volunteer staff worker for Al Gore. She did more volunteer work for Al than anyone I know. Karen was also a Gore delegate at the 2000 DNC, in Los Angeles, and managed to get me on the floor of the convention as an alternate delegate. Thanks to the late Jess O'Dear Jr., who was one of Al Gore's closest political friends. I gained much personal knowledge of Al Gore from Jess, and without him I could not have written this book.

Thanks to great friend Kenneth Grizzell for his spiritual advice and loyal support. Thanks to my godson Isaac Grizzell for being a great influence and inspiration. Thanks to my friend Joella Carr for her support and encouragement. She helped me tremendously by giving me the courage to continue to pursue this dream. Thanks to my longtime special friend Tina Carter for her advise, support, and encouragement. She was one of the first people to read the draft when the book idea was conceived in 1994. I want to thank my friend Sonny Elliott for the editing of photographs for the book. He is a great photographer. Thanks to my friend and lawyer Joey Taggert who been an invaluable advisor and friend. Thanks to my cousin Lisa McCord for her support and guidance. Without her helping to inspire and encourage me, there would be no book. There is no person more loyal and supportive than Lisa. And finally I want to thank my friend, agent, and Editor Walter McCord for his hard work and support. He was instrumental in helping to inspire me to continue my work, and gave me the encouragement to keep working when there were days I didn't feel like writing. He edited the first drafts (and there were many) of the book, patiently allowing me to write more words, before finally we had to stop due to time. He also made the initial contact with our publisher and negotiated the publishing contract. He is the most gifted agent and editor that I know and I owe him a great deal of gratitude and thanks. Thanks also to CJ my professional editor that the publisher hired on my behalf. CJ is an amazing editor and I thank you for making this book a much better read. Thanks to all of the referenced sources who contributed to this book. They are some of the best and brightest of the written word.

There are many people that I want to recognize who had a positive impact upon my life. Thanks to my parents, Claude and Helen Gipson, for all their love and support. They were the most caring parents anyone could have. Also thanks to my grandparents Claude and Jenny Gipson, who once hosted Albert Gore Sr. at their house, and my grandparents Albert and Estella Vaughn. My grandparents told me stories about Al Gore's father, and they were all strong Democrats and Gore supporters. Thanks to my sisters, Rhonda Dugas and Janice Brodioi, for their love and support, and to my brother-in-laws Roger Dugas and Joe Brodioi. Thanks to my nieces Tiffany Martin and Melissa Kennedy, and my nephew Jonathon Dugas.You all mean the world to me. Thanks also to all my aunts, uncles and cousins. They all had a very positive influence upon my life. Thanks to Uncle Osborne and Aunt Reba Baker for helping raise me. Thanks to my good friends Ricky Scharber, Monica Jones, Scotty Scharber, Johnny and Sarah Hunter, Sherry

Cowan-Greene, Eric Martin, Chris and Sonya Long, Mike Clayton, Brian Clayton, Mark Maybrey, Jackie Cheshire, Sandra Hoback, Tammy Kinningham, Gina Laxson-Jones, Janet Tabor, Barry Gosnell, Don Carver, Hunter Padar, Wally Cain, Sam Ingram, and Yancy and Jenny Weddington. They have always been loyal friends.

Thanks to Buddy Perry Sr. and Geraldine Perry for their friendship and help throughout the years, and to State Representative George Fraley and his wife Betty for their friendship and help during the years. They are the best and have done much work for the citizens of Middle Tennessee. Betty was a delegate for Al Gore in 2000, and I will always remember the great time we shared with other friends and longtime Gore supporters in Los Angeles during the 2000 DNC.

I would like to also thank many of my college professors, beginning with Dr. David Grubbs, political science professor and department chair at Middle Tennessee State University (MTSU). He was instrumental in my political science education. Also thanks to MTSU political science professors Dr. Everett Cunningham, Dr. Frank Essex, and Dr. Perez-Reilly. Thanks to my professors at Motlow State Community College in Tullahoma, Tennessee, including Dr. David Cheatham, Dr. Kay Clark, Dr. Helen White, and Dr. Weldon Payne. They each had a profound effect upon my college education and life in general. Dr. Weldon Payne taught me how to write like a reporter, and I will forever be grateful to him and all of my other professors. I was blessed to have the very best liberal arts professors anywhere, and that is a credit to both MTSU and Motlow State. Thanks also to Carey and Judy Wofford for their help and support during my internship with Al. They knew Al Gore as well as anyone, and both worked in his first congressional office in Winchester. I would like to acknowledge Bill Mason, Al Gore's former congressional district office manager and a former vice presidential staff member. He supervised me during my internship with Al Gore while I was attending college at MTSU. There are many more people to thank than I can possibly mention, but they, along with Al Gore, know who they are. Thanks to my Lord and Savior Jesus Christ for giving me more than I deserve. I have been truly blessed. God bless to all. Hope you like the book.

Troy Gipson

About the Author

Troy Gipson was born in Winchester, Tennessee, in 1961, and grew up in rural Franklin County, Tennessee. He spent his childhood riding tractors, playing baseball, shooting doves, collecting baseball cards, and asking questions. He became so adept at questioning things, that many people thought he would become a lawyer someday. Instead he became a political scientist. Gipson graduated from Middle Tennessee State University, in 1986, with a BS degree in political science, and Motlow State Community College, in 1983, with an AS degree in mass communications. While at Middle Tennessee State, he was elected Student Body Senior Senator and President of the College Young Democrats. He worked as a congressional intern in the Office of Congressman Albert Gore Jr. in 1981 and 1984-85. After graduating from college, he managed several political campaigns, and in 1988 Gipson was named Outstanding Young Person by the Franklin County, Tennessee, Jaycees. He was also honored by the Lions Club of Tennessee, in 1987, as a state finalist, for his public service work. From 1989 to 2009, Gipson worked for the Boeing Company, in Long Beach, California, and Huntsville Alabama, where he served as an internal auditor and property management specialist. While at Boeing he also served on the company's Property Council. He has written and published over fifty articles in *Politics Profile*, an Internet politics and news blog that he cofounded in 2011. In addition, he published an article for the *National Property Management Association* magazine in 2005. Gipson currently lives in Tennessee.

Endnotes

Chapter 1

1. *Time, August 21, 2000.*
2. Albert Gore, *An Inconvenient Truth (2006).*
3. Amy Lynch, *"Senator Superman"*, *Nashville Magazine, March 1985.*
4. Ibid.

Chapter 2

5. Albert Gore, *The Eye of the Storm,* (1970), 93-95. others selected.
6. Gore for Congress Campaign Brochure, 1976
7. Ibid
8. Tennessee Blue Book, 1978-79

Chapter 3

9. Al Gore Jr. Constitutional Oath in US House of Representatives, Fourth District of Tennessee, January 4, 1977 (Original Copy of Invitation).
10. Open Meeting – US Congressman Albert Gore, Jr., 1982 (Original Copy)
11. Mark Schwedt, *Tennessean,* April 25, 1982
12. Kevin Ellis, *Tennessean,* 1987
13. US Congressman Al Gore Jr. Meeting Announcement Letter, January 1979
14. Al Gore for Senate Campaign Newsletter, 1984 (Original Copy)
15. Congressional Record, October 1980 (Infant Formula Act)

16. Congressional Record, 1980 (Superfund Act)

17. Carolyn Shoulders, *Tennessean*. March 18, 1983

18. Carolyn Shoulders, *Tennessean*, November 18, 1983

19. Frank Gibson, *Tennessean*, December 15, 1981.

20. *Tennessean News Report*, August 18, 1982

21. Mike Shanahan, *Tennessean*, May 25, 1983

22. Albert Gore, Jr., "The Fork in the Road," *The New Republic*, May 5, 1982, 13-16

23. Ibid.

24. US Congressman Al Gore Jr., Meeting Announcement Letter, January 1983

25. Congressional Record, October 1984 (Organ Donor Network Act)

26. Adel Crowe, *Tennessean*, October 5, 1983.

27. Ibid.

28. Politics in America, 1984, *Congressional Quarterly Press*

Chapter 4

29. Ed Cromer, *Tennessean*, 1984. June 17, 1984.

30. Gore US Senate Campaign Newsletter, March 1984, (Original copy in files)

31. Personal notes from author

32. Jim O'Hara, *Tennessean*, October 7, 1984.

33. Gore US Senate Campaign Newsletter, June 1984

34. Al Gore, An Inconvient Truth (2006)

35. Carol Bradley, *Nashville Banner*, September 17, 1984

36. Carol Bradley and Bruce Dobie, *Nashville Banner*, November 5, 1984

Chapter 5

37. Pat Daly, *Tennessean*, Jan. 27, 1985.

38. Mike Pigott, *Nashville Banner*, June 11, 1985

39. Ibid.

40. Article by Senator Albert Gore Jr., 1986

41. Congressional Record, April 8, 1992.

42. Germond and Witcover Article, 1991
43. Patrick Willard, *Nashville Banner,* Oct. 6, 1990.
44. Ibid.
45. Congressional Record, May 10, 1990.
46. Congressional Record, July, 1989.
47. *Associated Press,* November 30, 1990
48. *Time,* November 6, 2000, and Congressional Record, January 12, 1991.

Chapter 6

49. *Tennessean, August 1987.*
50. *Tennessean,* 1987
51. *Tennessean,* 1987
52. Tennessean, 1987
53. *Associated Press,* September 29, 1987
54. *Tennessean,* January 5, 1988.
55. Tennessean, 1988
56. Jim O'Hara, *Tennessean, March 21, 1988.*
57. Jim O'Hara, *Tennessean,* April 16, 1988.
58. Bruce Dobie, *Nashville Banner,* April 1988.
59. Larry Daughtrey and Jim O'Hara, *Tennessean,* April 15, 1988.
60. Nashville Banner

Chapter 7

61. *Time,* July 20, 1992.
62. Albert Gore, *An Inconvenient Truth* (2006), 68-69.
63. *Time,* July 20, 1992, pg. 29
64. Al Gore, *An Inconvenient Truth,* 70.
65. Albert Gore, *Earth in the Balance (1992), 14.*
66. Al Gore, *Earth in the Balance.*
67. Ibid.
68. Gore, *Earth in the Balance (1992)*
69. Ibid.
70. Judy Keen, *USA Today,* May 21, 1991.

Chapter 8

71. *Time*
72. Bill Clinton, *My Life (2004), 414.*
73. Clinton-Gore Presidential Campaign Press Release, *July 16, 1992*
74. CPAN, *July 16,1992*
75. *CNN News Broadcas, 1992t*
76. *Ibid.*

Chapter 9

77.Bill Clinton, *My Life* (2004), 516.
78. Albert Gore, "Creating A Government that Works Better and Costs Less: Report of the National Performance Review," September 7, 1993
79. Ibid.
80. Wendy Walker, Producer, 2010
81. Ibid.
82. Hillary Rodham Clinton, *Living History*, 2003
83. US Congressional Record, September 1994
84. Clinton, *My Life*, 699
85. Personal Letters of Author

Chapter 10

86. Howard Fineman, *Newsweek*, May 24, 1999.
87. Richard L. Burke, *New York Times Magazine*, February 22, 1998.
88. Eric Pooley and Karen Tumulty, *Time*, December 15, 1997.
89. Bill Clinton, *My Life* (2004), 745–746.
90. *Tennessean*, December 14, 1997.
91. *Time*, December 15, 1997.
92. Eric Pooley and Karen Tumulty, *Time*, December 15, 1997.
93. Richard L. Burke, *The New York Times Magazine*, February 22, 1998
94. Richard L. Burke, *New York Times Magazine*, February 22, 1998
95. Susan Page, *USA Today*, June 22, 1998.

96. Ibid.
97. Larry Daughtrey, *Tennessean*, September 14, 1997.
98. Richard L. Burke, *The New York Times Magazine*, February 22, 1998
99. Mimi Hall, *USA Today*, May 26, 1999.
100. Ibid.
101. Howard Fineman, Time, May 24, 1999

Chapter 11

102. Eric Pooley, *Time*, August 21, 2000, 28
103. Theodore White, *The Making of the President* (1960),
104. *Time*, November 20, 2000.
105. Ibid.
106. Jeffrey Toobin, *Too Close to Call* (2001).
107. Ibid.
108. Ibid.
109. Ibid.
110. Ibid.
111. Lisa Munda, *The Washington Times Magazine*, Nov. 17, 2002, pg. 10.
112. Speech by Al Gore, December 13, 2000.
113. Palm Beach Post.
114. Ibid.
115. Al Gore, interview by Larry King, *Larry King Live*, CNN, November 19, 2002
116. Ibid.
117. Ibid.

Chapter 12

118. Kevin Sack, *New York Times*, January 25, 2001.
119. Richard L. Berke, *New York Times Magazine*, February 22, 1998
120. Ibid.
121. Al Gore, interview by Larry King, *Larry King Live*, CNN, November 19, 2002.
122. Apple Press Release, March 19, 2003.

123. Adam Nagourney, *New York Times*, December 15, 2002..
124. Boston.com. December 16, 2004.

Chapter 13

125. Al Gore, *An Inconvenient Truth* (2006).
126. Ibid.
127. Ibid.
128. Ibid.
129. Ibid.
130. Ibid.
131. Ibid.
132. Steve Gorman, *Los Angeles Times*, February 26, 2007.
133. Eric Pooley, *Time*, May 16, 2007.
134. The Nobel Foundation, 2007.
135. Bono, *Time*, December 19, 2007.

Chapter 14

136. Eric Pooley, *Time*, May 16, 2007.
137. Al Gore, *The Assault on Reason* (2007).
138. The Climate Reality Project, 2011
139. ABC News, November 3, 2009.
140. Al Gore, *Our Choice* (2009), Introduction.
141. Al Gore. *Our Choice*. 2009.
142. Al Gore, *Rolling Stone*, June 22, 2011.
143. Ibid.
144. Walt Mossberg and Peter Kafka, *All Things D*, October 20, 2011.

Epilogue

1. Al Gore, *The Assault on Reason*, 2007.
2. Larry King, *CNN Larry King Live* 2002.
3. Al Gore, *The Assault on Reason*, 2007.
4. Ibid.

Source Notes
Chapter One
This chapter is based on my exclusive conversations with Vice President Al Gore (January-February 2010). It is also based on the referenced sources cited in the Endnotes section of book. In addition, many parts of the book are based upon my personal knowledge of the subject.

Chapter Two
This chapter is based on based on the referenced sources cited in the Endnotes section of book along with my own personal knowledge of the subject. In addition I had interviews and conversations with Jess O'Dear Sr.

Chapter Three
This chapter is based on based on the referenced sources cited in the Endnotes section of book along with my own personal knowledge of the subject. In addition I conducted interviews and conversations with Jess O'Dear Sr. and Claude Gipson Jr. I also recorded personal notes from my internship with Congressman Al Gore Jr.

Chapter Four
This chapter is based on based on the referenced sources cited in the Endnotes section of book along with my own personal knowledge of the subject. I also recorded personal notes during my internship with Congressman Al Gore Jr. from 1984 to 1985. In addition I had interviews and conversations with Jess O'Dear Sr. and Claude Gipson Jr.

Chapter Five
This chapter is based on based on the referenced sources cited in the Endnotes section of book along with my own personal knowledge of the subject.

Chapter Six
This chapter is based on based on the referenced sources cited in the Endnotes section of book along with my own personal knowledge of

the subject. In addition I recorded personal notes and information files from the Al Gore Presidential Campaign of 1988.

Chapter Seven
This chapter is based on based on the referenced sources cited in the Endnotes section of book along with my own personal knowledge of the subject. In addition I recorded personal notes and information files, and recorded television videos.

Chapter Eight
This chapter is based on based on the referenced sources cited in the Endnotes section of book along with my own personal knowledge of the subject. In addition I recorded personal notes and information files, and viewed television videos.

Chapter Nine
This chapter is based on based on the referenced sources cited in the Endnotes section of book along with my own personal knowledge of the subject. In addition I recorded personal notes and information files, and viewed television videos from CNN News.

Chapter Ten
This chapter is based on based on the referenced sources cited in the Endnotes section of book along with my own personal knowledge of the subject. In addition I recorded personal notes and information files, and viewed television videos from CNN News.

Chapter Eleven
This chapter is based on based on the referenced sources cited in the Endnotes section of book along with my own personal knowledge of the subject. In addition I conducted interviews and conversations with Karen Garner. In addition I recorded personal notes and information files, and viewed television videos from CNN News.

Chapter Twelve
This chapter is based on based on the referenced sources cited in the Endnotes section of book along with my own personal knowledge of the subject.

Chapter Thirteen
This chapter is based on based on the referenced sources cited in the Endnotes section of book along with my own personal knowledge of the subject.

Chapter Fourteen
This chapter is based on my exclusive conversations with Vice President Al Gore (January-February 2010). It is also based on the referenced sources cited in the Endnotes section of book along with my own personal knowledge and notes.

Appendix

This section of the book is based on the referenced sources cited.

Epilogue

This chapter is based on based on the referenced sources cited in the Endnotes section of book along with my own personal knowledge of the subject.

Photos

All photos in this book are the exclusive rights of the author and/or Vice President Gore. Several of the photos in the book were provided by Vice President Gore's office for use in the book and are copyrighted.

29318604R00137

Made in the USA
Charleston, SC
09 May 2014